LOUIS COMFORT TIFFANY

Louis Comfort Tiffany

ALASTAIR DUNCAN

Harry N. Abrams, Inc., Publishers, New York

IN ASSOCIATION WITH

The National Museum of American Art, Smithsonian Institution

Series Editor: Margaret L. Kaplan
Editor: Eve Sinaiko
Designer: Ellen Nygaard Ford
Photo Research: Neil Ryder Hoos

Library of Congress Cataloging-in-Publication Data

Duncan, Alastair, 1942–
    Louis Comfort Tiffany / Alastair Duncan.
        p.   cm. — (Library of American art)
    Includes bibliographical references and index.
    ISBN 0–8109–3862–6
    1. Tiffany, Louis Comfort, 1848–1933.   2. Glassware—United
States—History—19th century.   3. Glassware—United States—
History—20th century.   4. Glassworkers—United States—Biography.
    I. Title.   II. Series: Library of American art (Harry N. Abrams, Inc.)
NK5198.T5D86   1992
748'.092—dc20   92–4702
                                                                   CIP

Frontispiece: *Dragonfly table lamp.* c. 1900–1910. See page 102.

Text copyright © 1992 Alastair Duncan
Illustrations copyright © 1992 Harry N. Abrams, Inc.

Published in 1992 by Harry N. Abrams, Incorporated, New York

A Times Mirror Company

Printed and bound in Japan

Contents

Paperweight vase

Acknowledgments

Gratitude is extended to the following individuals and institutions whose generous assistance in providing information and photographs has made the compilation of this book possible: Richard Goodbody and David Robinson (principal photography); Betsy Arvidson, National Academy of Design, New York; David Bellis; Frederick R. Brandt, Virginia Museum of Fine Arts, Richmond; Brooklyn Museum, New York; Thomas Burke Memorial Washington State Museum, University of Washington, Seattle; David Burlingham; Michael J. Burlingham; Jay Cantor; Christie's Fine Art Auctioneers, New York; Corning Museum of Glass, Corning, New York; John D'Agostino; John and Miyoko Davey; Howie and Paula Ellman; William Gerdes; Neil Harris, University of Chicago; Hirshhorn Museum and Sculpture Garden, Smithsonian Institution, Washington, D.C.; John Howat, Metropolitan Museum of Art, New York; Indianapolis Museum of Art, Indiana; Gregory Kuharic, Sotheby's, Inc., New York; Bradley Larson, Oshkosh Public Museum, Wisconsin; Museum of Modern Art, New York; National Museum of American History, Smithsonian Institution, Washington, D.C.; The New-York Historical Society; Ophir Gallery, Englewood, New Jersey; Julie Parson, Chicago Public Library; Jon Peters; Raymond Petke, Wadsworth Atheneum, Hartford, Connecticut; Henry B. Platt; Mrs. Louise Lusk Platt; Colonel and Mrs. Jake Rudd; Joel Schur; Sheldon Memorial Art Gallery, University of Nebraska, Lincoln; Ira Simon; Team Antiques, Great Neck, New York; Mr. and Mrs. Roy Warshawsky; Barbara Weinberg, Metropolitan Museum of Art, New York; Wilmington Society of Fine Arts, Delaware Art Center; and Janet Zapata. Very special thanks are extended to MaryBeth McCaffrey for her research and coordination of the entire project.

ALASTAIR DUNCAN

Paperweight vase

c. 1905–10. Favrile glass, 8″ high
Inscribed *L.C.T. 7106A*, and with the
firm's original paper label
Private collection

For commentary, see page 92.

Louis Comfort Tiffany as a student

Introduction

THE SHEER VOLUME OF PRODUCTS GENERATED by the Tiffany Studios for so many years has overwhelmed the public's perception of the man at the heart of this great commercial enterprise; one whose prodigious talents as an artist were channeled into, and finally veiled by, his attempt to shape mass consumer taste in America. Under the stewardship of Louis Comfort Tiffany, Tiffany Studios became, in effect, a consortium of industrial designers producing a clearly defined and highly personalized range of household goods marketed aggressively through press releases, advertisements, sales brochures, and domestic and international expositions.

Yet Tiffany was never fully comfortable with his role as an entrepreneur and for this reason never allowed it fully to camouflage, or finally to extinguish, his career as an artist. It was the latter that had first fueled his ambitions to bring beauty into every home and that led, in turn, to the mass production that this engendered. In fact, the issue of how to juggle his two roles—that of artist and that of industrial designer—remained a dilemma with which he wrestled for more than fifty years, and one that he never resolved to his complete satisfaction.

Tiffany remains an elusive and enigmatic figure. Despite the celebrity of the family name—forged for posterity as much by him as by his father's renowned New York store, Tiffany & Company—practically nothing is known of Tiffany beyond, or apart from, his art. Even after the explosion of interest in his works by collectors in the 1970s and 1980s, and the often frenetic search for information about him that this has generated by historians, there remains little by which to assess the personal ambitions behind his giant accomplishments.

Born on February 18, 1848, to privilege and wealth, Tiffany declined the security of a university education and employment in the family firm for an independent career in the arts. His early schooling—first at the Flushing Academy on Long Island, and then at the Eagleswood Military Academy in Perth Amboy, New Jersey—was undistinguished. He was reported to be headstrong and to loathe schoolwork; characteristics common, no doubt, to most of his classmates.

Photographs taken of him later—attired fastidiously in three-piece

Louis Comfort Tiffany as a student at the Eagleswood Military Academy, Perth Amboy, New Jersey

c. 1864. Courtesy of the Mitchell-Tiffany Papers, The Sterling Memorial Library, Manuscripts and Archives Division, Yale University, New Haven, Connecticut

In a letter to his sister, Annie, in 1862, the fourteen-year-old Tiffany complained of the discipline imposed on him at Eagleswood, to which his parents had sent him, as he had shown himself previously to be headstrong and a poor student.

9

suits that suggest the profession of banker or physician rather than that of artist—reveal nothing in his bearded countenance of the fierce inner drive and voracious appetite for work that became the dominant traits of his long and diverse career. His first biographer, Charles de Kay, provided a fitting and succinct testimonial to these aspects of his personality: "Infinite, endless labor makes the masterpiece."

In later life, when pressed on his many successes, Tiffany invariably spoke with diffidence of his continuing role as a student of art. In a 1916 speech published in *International Studio* magazine, he said, "If I may be forgiven a word about my own work, I would merely say that I have always striven to fix beauty in wood or stone or glass or pottery, in oil or water color, by using whatever seemed fittest by the expression of beauty; that has been my creed, and I see no reason to change it." At other times, he spoke expansively of issues relating to the works that he had created, of the aesthetic concepts that had motivated him, but never of his own contribution to their creation. It becomes apparent, despite the dearth of surviving personal information on him, that he set standards for himself above and beyond the comprehension of others, that his artistic agenda was self-imposed and self-regulated, and that he intended to live through, and be judged by, his work. His ambitions, finally, were somehow other-worldly and messianic. As he wrote in an article, "The Quest of Beauty," his goal was to harness in everyday objects "the endless wealth of precept and suggestion . . . in air and water and earth, in all the vast, teeming bosom of nature."

Inextricably bound to his attempt to beautify his surroundings was Tiffany's preoccupation with perfection. Stories have survived through the families of his top employees, such as Joseph Briggs and Frederick Wilson, of him as an old man walking through the factory in Corona, New York, and striking with his cane pieces from the workbench that did not meet his artistic or technical standards of the moment. Other anecdotes corroborate this image of a man obsessed with excellence, which on occasion manifested itself negatively in his relationship with his staff. Tiffany could be an arbitrary, high-handed, and uncompromising employer, one who was equally prepared to overrule his clients on artistic issues. Other than in this blind obsession with quality, which kept those around him constantly on the alert, Tiffany appears to have been considerate and generous to his employees, responding readily to their financial and family needs. His own family—specifically, his children—likewise loved and revered him, but with distinctly similar reservations. In effect, they remembered him as much for his strictness and authoritarianism as for his parental love. Dorothy, the youngest of his six children, recalled in a 1978 interview with her grandson, Michael John Burlingham (published in *The Last Tiffany*, 1989), that she and her siblings viewed him as eccentric, even at the height of his fame and creativity at the turn of the century. As in the Corona workshops, no tolerance was given in the home for carelessness or unpunctuality. Tiffany's disciplinary obsessions increased further after the death of his second wife, Louise, in 1904, when he succumbed to bouts of deep depression and even, briefly, to nocturnal drinking. Barely

Tiffany with his first wife, Mary, and their children, Mary, Charles Lewis II, and Hilda, c. 1880.

It can be difficult, in such period group photographs, to identify the Tiffany children, because boys and girls at the time often wore identical clothes and haircuts.

in her teens when her mother died, Dorothy sought his affection desperately. For his part, Tiffany took solace in solitude, distancing himself from those around him and plunging more deeply into his work. Perhaps he is best described, in sum, as a benevolent autocrat.

The extraordinary growth and prosperity enjoyed by America toward the turn of the century proved fortunate for Tiffany, affording him

unique opportunities to expand his business and to capitalize on the nation's first Gilded Age. The country was in a self-indulgent and celebratory mood, and it spent lavishly. Tiffany quickly positioned himself as its most fashionable purveyor of taste, not only within the home, but in every type of public and private institution, including churches, hotels, clubs, libraries, and hospitals. Soon his intoxicating blend of colors and designs, rendered in combinations of glass, bronze, enamels, and other materials, became the era's proudest and most identifiable decorative imprimatur; Americans who sought to be fashionable simply could not do without it.

Today we can only marvel at the stupefying volume and versatility of what Tiffany created. He did not excel in every attempt, nor was he equally skilled in all the mediums he essayed, but he left an incomparable legacy, unique in its unapologetic orgy of colors and its worship of nature.

Self-Portrait

I. The Early Careers:
Painting and Interior Design

MANY OF TIFFANY'S FINEST PAINTINGS have been retained within his family: the Burlinghams, Platts, Lusks, Gilders, and others. This has slowed the general public's ability fully to judge his talents as an artist. Works on canvas and paper by him are often unremarkable, if not drab, North African genre paintings of Arab souks and desert landscapes; although these reach the marketplace intermittently through public auction, there remains for most Tiffany enthusiasts the hope that they are unrepresentative of an artist who could create such spectacular beauty in other disciplines. It is a common belief that somehow he *had* to be an accomplished painter too. The retrospective of his paintings held in 1979 at the Grey Art Gallery, New York University, offered the public the chance finally to evaluate Tiffany's career as a painter; it included a comprehensive selection of works owned by his descendants and others from private collections and institutions, such as the Morse Museum of American Art, in Winter Park, Florida, and the Yale University Art Gallery in New Haven, Connecticut. Suddenly, discussion shifted from his possible weaknesses as a painter to his undeniable strengths.

Part of the difficulty in attempting to assess Tiffany's paintings and to compare them critically with those of his contemporaries lies in the fact that his style defies exact categorization. Whereas he was in many ways in the mainstream of that generation of American painters whose careers were launched immediately after the Civil War, not only did he follow at some distance the changes that were introduced, but he did so with a distinctly personal interpretation. Although, for example, most landscapists from 1866 on rejected the photographic realism and vast and majestic panoramic views embraced by Albert Bierstadt, Thomas Cole, and Frederick Edwin Church in favor of compositions that were less detailed and ambitious in scale, Tiffany's renderings of the outdoors were still more soft-edged and intimate than most, their impact depending less on form or subject matter than on light and color. It was this last-mentioned, finally, that became the dominating factor in his works on canvas and later in glass.

Self-Portrait

c. 1872. Oil on canvas, mounted on Masonite,
20 x 16"
Unsigned
The National Academy of Design, New York

Presented by Tiffany to the National Academy of Design in 1872, the year after he was elected an associate of the Academy, this is the only recorded self-portrait by the artist. It provides a rare view of him as an adult without a beard.

15

View of the Palisades, New Jersey

The cliff has been identified. It stands about one and one-half miles north of Alpine, New Jersey, on the west bank of the Hudson River. Both the subject matter of the painting and its emphasis on bright outdoor light show the influence of George Inness in Tiffany's early work.

Examination of Tiffany's formal training as a painter (or, perhaps more pertinently, his lack of it) and of the artistic influences to which he responded helps to explain the circumstances surrounding his later decision to explore other fields of artistic expression. In March 1866, following his first trip to Europe, during which he had filled a small sketchbook with studies of the places he visited, Tiffany announced to his family his intention to study art rather than attend college. This was against the wish of his father, who had expected him, as the scion, to enter the family firm. Notwithstanding, Charles Lewis Tiffany was persuaded to provide financial support, and Louis was enrolled at the National Academy of Design in New York for the academic year of 1866–67, for what was to be the only formal instruction that he ever received.

Charles de Kay noted in *The Art Work of Louis C. Tiffany* that he was inspired more beyond the classroom than in it, particularly by his introduction to the painter George Inness, whose studio on Washington Square he began to frequent around 1867. The relationship was casual, with Inness providing "incisive, outspoken views on art...supplemented

PAINTING AND INTERIOR DESIGN

by a stimulating if somewhat chaotic philosophy.... Inness did not give instruction in painting; his way was to criticise or appreciate the work of a young artist from time to time."

Inness's particular importance to Tiffany was that he was a Tonalist and, as such, depicted his landscapes in a soft and mystical manner achieved through the subtle modulation of a narrow range of colors. Like Homer Dodge Martin, Dwight W. Tryon, and the other Tonalists of the period, Inness sought a highly personal interpretation of nature, one concerned less with form and detail than with the attempt, simply, to evoke in the viewer an emotional response. Samuel Isham, in *The History of American Painting*, quotes Inness on this idea: "The purpose of the painter is simply to reproduce in other minds the impression which a scene has made upon him. A work of art does not appeal to the intellect. It does not appeal to the moral sense. Its aim is not to instruct, not to edify, but to awaken an emotion." Tiffany concentrated his energies during the next few years on trips to Europe and on exhibiting, upon his returns to New York, the canvases that he had painted there. During a sojourn in Paris

Roccabrunna

Undated. Oil on canvas, 15⅜ x 24⅜″
Signed lower left
Wadsworth Atheneum, Hartford. Ella Gallup
Sumner and Mary Catlin Sumner Collection

Roquebrune is in France, on the Route de la Grande-Corniche, the road that runs between Nice and Genoa on the Riviera. The town's steep elevation, distinct rock formations, and ruined tenth-century castle have proved a popular subject with landscape artists.

Italian Landscape

1870s. Oil on canvas, mounted on fiberboard,
21¼ x 16¼"
Signed lower left
Hirshhorn Museum and Sculpture Garden,
Washington, D.C.
Gift of Joseph H. Hirshhorn, 1972

It appears that Tiffany visited Italy several times from the early 1870s on. Of an unidentified location, the painting corresponds in terrain to that in other canvases listed by Tiffany as Piedmontese.

around 1868, he studied briefly under Léon-Charles-Adrien Bailly in his Passy atelier. Bailly was a strict academician who advocated a rigorous training schedule to ensure that young artists mastered the fundamentals of their métier; long hours of drawing from both live models and plaster casts preceded their attempts to work in color directly on the canvas. Through either disinterest or a lack of discipline, Tiffany declined this opportunity—possibly his last—to hone his skills as a draftsman and to learn how to draw the human form, an omission that is often evident in his figural paintings. His renderings of people and animals are, in many

PAINTING AND INTERIOR DESIGN

instances, awkward and stiff, suggesting a sense of uncertainty in their execution. Bodies do not appear fully modeled, nor do their individual parts always connect naturally. Tiffany was clearly aware of his limitations as a portraitist, and drew many of his figures with their faces turned away from, or invisible to, the viewer.

In addition to the canvases he painted overseas, Tiffany completed at this time a series of local landscapes, including views of the Hudson River, that were noteworthy for their wide, picturesque format and qualities of light and moisture-laden atmosphere. His technique was consistent with that of most of his peers: a sketch was made on site and completed from memory in his studio. At this time he also began to use photographs, which he himself took, in the preparation of his canvases, as these were helpful in framing and organizing the composition.

Tiffany's busy travel and exhibition schedule continued in the early 1870s, when he participated in about twenty-seven shows, and traveled extensively in Europe and the Near East. At some point during this time he met Samuel Colman, a painter (and later associate) who, like Inness, exerted a great influence on him in his formative years. Colman was a landscapist in the tradition of the Hudson River school whose canvases revealed a greater fidelity to nature than those of Inness. They had a certain firmness of outline and delicate detailing, and he loved warm, pure colors; these were qualities that appealed also to Tiffany.

A Family Row on the Hudson

c. 1872. Oil on canvas, mounted on Masonite, 10 x 17⅝" Signed lower left New Jersey State Museum, Trenton. Museum purchase

Characteristic of Tiffany's early renderings of the Hudson River valley, the composition allows ample manipulation of light and color in its broad expanse of sky and water. Tiffany's treatment here is similar to that employed at the time by Samuel Colman and the group of painters known as the Tonalists. The painting was displayed at the Brooklyn Museum in 1872.

Market Scene in Geneva

On a subsequent trip to Europe, Tiffany was reunited with Colman in Spain, and from there the two crossed to North Africa and traveled through Morocco, Algeria, Tunisia, and Egypt. Tiffany translated his impressions into intimate street and harbor scenes and small oil and watercolor studies done from life, while Colman's canvases portrayed sweeping views of the desert, itinerant camel caravans, and archaeological sites. Both used dramatic color techniques, such as the interplay of light and shadow, to achieve their intended effects.

North Africa exerted a profound influence on Tiffany's eye and art, so much so that he arranged to study briefly in Paris under Léon-Adolphe-Auguste Belly, a noted French landscapist who, like Jean-Léon Gérôme and Eugène Fromentin, had developed a reputation as an Orientalist while traveling in North Africa and the Levant. At the time, Tiffany's infatuation with the region was shared by several other young American painters, including Edwin Lord Weeks, Charles Sprague Pearce, and H. Siddons Mowbray, who were similarly drawn to its unique mix of exoticism, daunting vistas, and penetrating sunlight. In a 1917 address before the Rembrandt Club of Brooklyn, later published in the journal *The Art World,* Tiffany recalled the impact of his first trip to North Africa: "When first I had a chance to travel in the East and to paint where the people and the buildings also are clad in beautiful hues, the pre-eminence of color in the world was brought forcibly to my attention. I returned to New York wondering why we made so little use of our eyes, why we refrained so obstinately from taking advantage of color in our

Market Scene in Geneva

1874. Watercolor on paper, 20 x 13⅓"
Signed lower right and inscribed GENEVA AUG 30, 74
Collection of William R. Gerdes,
Queensbury, New York

Tiffany painted several charming market scenes in Europe, some of the finest of which, such as Marketplace at Nuremburg, *have remained within his family. This example is typical of most in its placement of the vendors and their wares in the foreground of a tree-shaded square. Characteristic also is his rendition of the figures with their faces turned downward or away from the viewer, both means whereby he did not have to define their features in detail.*

Market Day outside the Walls of
Tangier, Morocco

1873. Oil on canvas, 35 x 56"
Signed lower left
The National Museum of American Art,
Smithsonian Institution, Washington, D.C.

architecture and our clothing when Nature indicates its mastership." In the same article, "Color and Its Kinship to Sound," Tiffany further acknowledged his debt to the Near East in its arousal and development of his own color instincts: "The Orientals have been teaching the Occidentals how to use colors for the past 10,000 years or so.... The men of the East who supplied barbarians with rugs and figured textiles considered color first, and form only incidentally. Their designs were spots or tracts of color, and during the course of time they learned through reasoning and instinct that a fine design can be spoilt if the wrong combinations and juxtaposition of colors are chosen. We have to discover, as they did, what marvelous power one color has over another, and what the relative size of each different tract of color means to the result—what the mass of each different color means for the effect of the design as a whole!"

Throughout the 1870s, Tiffany drew a certain admiration from his painting colleagues, due in part to his boundless energy and optimism. Various honors were bestowed on him, including his election, at the age of twenty-two, as an associate member of the National Academy of Design, and membership in the American Watercolor Society, which had been formed in 1866 under the name of the American Society of Painters in Watercolors. In 1876 he exhibited three oils and five watercolors at the Philadelphia Centennial Exposition (six of which were of Middle Eastern scenes), and the following year joined Inness, Augustus Saint-Gaudens, Thomas Eakins, Albert Pinkham Ryder, John Singer Sargent, James McNeill Whistler, and John La Farge, among others, in the formation of the Society of American Artists (Tiffany was elected its first treasurer). This was a vehicle for the display and promotion of progressive trends in

Market Day outside the Walls of Tangier, Morocco. Photograph from Tiffany's personal album, 1873, inscribed, on reverse, Tangiers, May 5th market day. Collection of the Charles Hosmer Morse Museum of American Art, Winter Park, Florida.

Like many of his artist colleagues, Tiffany found that the camera assisted him greatly. Photographs could be used later to ensure the accuracy of a canvas that he had begun while on his travels, but preferred to complete at his convenience, upon his return home. Although this photograph was taken at a different angle from that of the painting, it provides a clear record of the various elements in the composition, and of their interrelationship.

*On the Way between Old and
New Cairo, Citadel Mosque of
Mohammed Ali and Tombs of the
Mamelukes*

c. 1872. Oil on canvas, 41½ x 68″
Signed lower left
The Brooklyn Museum, New York.
Gift of George Foster Peabody

One of Tiffany's largest and most dramatic Orientalist canvases, this depiction of a caravan passing in front of some of Cairo's most spectacular landmarks provides strongly contrasting colors and sharp perspectives. Exhibited at the National Academy of Design in 1872, the painting has on occasion drawn criticism for the static appearance of the approaching travelers and their camels. Nevertheless, it reveals Tiffany's taste for exotic and graceful architectural forms, such as the ogival domes pictured here.

Walled City, North Africa

1870s. Watercolor on paper, 25½ x 39½"
Signed lower left
Private collection

Here Tiffany has used the juncture of the curved roadway in the foreground with the horizontal walls of the city to balance the composition. It is the central stepped row of stark white buildings, however, that immediately draws the eye, reminding the viewer of Tiffany's continuing search for dramatic light effects in his work.

Duane Street, New York

Tin Peddler at Sea Bright,
New Jersey

c. 1888. Oil on mounted board, 22¾ x 29⅛"
Signed lower left
Private collection

Tiffany composed this painting from several photographs that he himself took of a peddler offering his wares (now in the collection of the Morse Museum of American Art, Winter Park, Florida). Like many late-nineteenth-century artists, Tiffany utilized the camera both as a means to frame his compositions on canvas and as a visual record for the time when he later completed them. This painting was exhibited at the American Watercolor Society in 1889.

American art, one intended to present a challenge to the conservative National Academy of Design, which refused to show the works of many younger artists. In 1878 Tiffany exhibited three canvases at the Exposition Universelle in Paris; one of these, titled *Duane Street, New York,* anticipated, in its depiction of urban squalor, the Ash Can school, although the social commentary implicit in the latter's work was absent. Tiffany often painted unromantic locales, such as slum housing, but he had no personal opinions to express in doing so.

In 1880, when he had already begun to explore other fields of artistic expression (L. C. Tiffany & Associated Artists had been formed the preceding year), Tiffany was elected a full member of the National Academy of Design. By this time he was perceived as a painter apart; one well received, but whose style was undefinable by the standard criteria used to define art schools and movements.

In the 1880s, as interest in French Impressionism spread and Claude Monet's American disciples, such as J. Alden Weir and Theodore Robinson, made pilgrimages to Giverny, Tiffany applied the style's concepts to a series of *plein-air* family portraits that he drew at the Tiffanys' Irvington-on-Hudson estate. The canvases, which were rendered in a high-keyed palette, with broken brushwork and flattened perspectives, are enchanting, and remind the viewer of how Tiffany later summarized his paintings: "One instance in time, a fragment of a happy day, nothing more."

Duane Street, New York

c. 1878. Oil on canvas, 27 x 30"
Signed lower left
The Brooklyn Museum, New York.
Dick S. Ramsay Fund

One of three canvases that Tiffany exhibited at the 1878 Exposition Universelle in Paris, this painting captures one of the harsher realities of the Industrial Revolution: urban squalor. Unlike the later Ash Can school artists, however, Tiffany painted this and other views of depressed city life without attempting to offer an accompanying social commentary.

At Irvington-on-Hudson

c. 1879. Oil on canvasboard, 18½ x 24½"
Signed lower left
Sheldon Memorial Art Museum,
University of Nebraska, Lincoln. Nebraska Art
Association-Nelle Cochrane Woods Memorial
Collection, 1972. N-279

The two people in the painting are probably Tiffany's first wife, Mary, and their daughter Hilda. Strongly reminiscent of Monet's impressionistic renderings of figures in flower-bedecked meadows, this appears to be the canvas Tiffany exhibited at the National Academy of Design in 1879 with the title At Irvington.

Family Group with Cow

c. 1888. Oil on canvas, 28¾ x 29⅜"
Signed lower left
Private collection

This painting is a sequel to one titled My Family at Somesville *in the collection of the Morse Museum of American Art. The group presumably shows, from left, Tiffany's daughter Mary, with one of the twins, Hilda, Charles Lewis II, and Tiffany's second wife, Louise, on an outing in Somesville, Maine. Somesville is a resort area on Mount Desert Island on the Maine coast.*

Other outdoor genre paintings that he executed in the Impressionist style were composed of broad brushstrokes to define single forms or background areas and agitated ones to depict jumbled detailing, such as vegetables in a field or meadow. One such painting, *The Harvesters* (c. 1879, see page 32), borrowed shamelessly from Jean-François Millet for its composition and tonality.

Tiffany continued to paint throughout his life, but his increasing preoccupation, from the mid-1880s on, with his glass operations reduced both the volume and quality of his painted works. His principal ambition—to re-create in his art nature's infinite spectrum—led him inexorably to the perfection of a new and inimitable type of glasswork, one that became a far superior vehicle for the creation of color than a painter's easel and canvas.

It is impossible to deduce precisely the moment when Tiffany's commitment to painting—that is, to a full-time career in it—began to wane. His curiosity about other art forms was evident from the mid-1870s, but whether this was the natural outgrowth of his innate restlessness and boundless energy, or the conscious search for an alternative vocation, is unclear. Convention records that he moved effortlessly from painting to interior design, which in tandem became essential building blocks on the way to his final career, that of consummate glass artist and designer. In reality, however, the evolution was probably far less systematic than the biographers who espouse this theory would have the reader believe. In all probability Tiffany did not, as Candace Wheeler recalled in her 1918 book, *Yesterdays in a Busy Life,* go into decorative work solely because he believed that "there is more to it than in painting pictures...it is the real thing, you know; a business, not a philanthropy or an amateur educational scheme. We are going after the money there is in art, but art is there, after all."

Common sense points to the likelihood of a different interpretation: that any artist trained in the fine arts—by the definition of the time either painting or sculpture—would consider the professions of interior design and window making less esteemed than his own, and that Tiffany must therefore have been persuaded to make the change in part through disillusionment with painting, or, more exactly, with his status in the field. Although of surpassing ability as a landscapist and colorist, he must have known by 1875 that he could not aspire to the top rung as an artist, that his technical shortcomings, lack of formal instruction, and academic nonconformity—factors evident singly or in combination in much of his oeuvre—would deny him that distinction. In the 1870s, several American painters of his generation—for example, Frank D. Millet, Albert Pinkham Ryder, Frank Duveneck, Dwight W. Tryon, and Edwin Blashfield—

PAINTING AND INTERIOR DESIGN

were perceived as more accomplished, and it was predictable therefore that someone with Tiffany's ambitions would begin to explore other avenues through which to excel and establish his reputation. That there was within the artistic community at the time a new awareness of, and dialogue with, the applied arts no doubt helped to ease his impending transition, yet he did not move directly from painting into the field of the decorative arts (as had La Farge), but first into that of interior design. Then, as now, this was clearly not a logical alternative choice for a disenchanted painter, even though it offered him access to the country's foremost architects and patrons with wealth—two elements essential to the window-making business that he soon established. Nevertheless, the move appears, in retrospect, to have been beneficial, providing valuable experience and contacts on which he would later draw. At the time, however, Tiffany must have pondered its suitability and purpose.

Tiffany's interest in the decorative arts was first piqued by Edward C. Moore, the general manager and chief silverware designer of Tiffany & Company, who was also a collector of Oriental and Near Eastern artifacts. The 1876 Centennial Exposition in Philadelphia probably drew Tiffany's attention further to the applied arts, as it generated a heated debate over the American furniture exhibits, which were seen, in juxtaposition with those mounted by English and European manufacturers, to have been inspired directly by them, and therefore to be lacking in originality. Tiffany's friend and mentor, and his sister Annie's brother-in-law, Donald G. Mitchell, was chairman of judges for the decorative-arts section of the exposition, and Tiffany no doubt became familiar through him with the enormous volume of discussion and concern that the issue raised.

Two other acquaintances were instrumental in attracting Tiffany to the virtues of the applied arts: Samuel Colman, who was a collector of rare textiles, and Candace Wheeler, an embroiderer and specialist in textile and needlework production. Tiffany was also influenced by Lockwood De Forest, the son of an attorney for Tiffany & Company, who was a collector of Indian artifacts and was himself an artist. In assessing the dearth of creativity among American craftsmen, the four clearly saw a need in New York's high society for a team of bright young artist-designers to decorate and furnish the homes of the wealthy in a smart and innovative manner. The decision was therefore made, in 1879, to form an interior design firm, which was named L. C. Tiffany & Associated Artists. Included in the partnership were Tiffany, Wheeler, Colman, and De Forest; the last-mentioned appears to have participated as a consultant on matters relating to wood carving and its ornamentation.

Although the four had specific skills and responsibilities, Tiffany was the dominant force, as it was his family's social status and wealth that

The Harvesters

provided them with the necessary introduction into New York society. This, in addition to the fact that he was more urbane and cosmopolitan than the others, and had more energy and optimism, made him their automatic leader and spokesman. Nevertheless, he did find the time to pursue other interests, including painting and glass experimentation, the latter hampered in the 1870s by two successive fires that destroyed the kiln he had installed in his home, forcing him to rent time at commercial glasshouses.

The business was launched by the immediate commission to provide a drop curtain for the Madison Square Theater in New York, at the invitation of the theater's owner, Steele MacKaye. This, appropriately for the new venture, became a joint effort: Tiffany was responsible for the overall design (a landscape with flowers), Colman for the choice of colors, De Forest for that of the materials, and Wheeler for the supervision of the curtain's execution.

Next, and far more auspicious, were the commissions to furnish and decorate a salon in the residence of George Kemp, a wealthy New York pharmaceutical supplier, at 720 Fifth Avenue, and two rooms in the Seventh Regimental Armory, on Park Avenue at Sixty-seventh Street, the new home of the Knickerbocker Greys.

Contemporary views of the Kemp salon reveal several elements that quickly became part of the firm's decorative repertoire: walls with flat, patterned designs, exotic hanging lamps, a fireplace with a tiled-glass surround, painted friezes, leaded-glass transoms, and furnishings in the style that is today broadly defined as the Aesthetic Movement. To its proponents, such an effect was unorthodox, fresh, and imaginative; to its detractors, discordant, a trifle jumbled, and lacking in architectural integrity.

The commission for the Seventh Regimental Armory followed that for Kemp shortly, and was completed by September 1880. The firm was retained to decorate two public spaces: a Veterans Room and a library. With Stanford White, of the firm of McKim, Mead & White, as his architectural consultant, Tiffany set out to produce settings that would venerate history's epic battles and the majesty of the military experience. One of the few Tiffany interiors to have survived largely intact, the Veterans Room is of special interest to today's Tiffany historian. Although the room's original mood and color scheme have gone—due, in part, to the inevitable fading and disintegration through the years of its textiles, and their subsequent removal—enough of the original interior has remained to permit the viewer to assess the aesthetic impact sought by Tiffany and his colleagues. Included were four window hangings in mixed colors and textures; a portière in Japanese brocade (all now destroyed); a monumen-

The Harvesters

c. 1879. Oil on canvas, 17½ x 23½"
Signed lower left
Private collection

Exhibited at the National Academy of Design, this is one of a series of compositions on the theme of harvesting that Tiffany completed during the late 1870s and early 1880s. It is clearly influenced by a similar series painted earlier by Jean-François Millet in the French countryside.

The dining room in the residence of George Kemp at 720 Fifth Avenue, New York, c. 1879. As in so many of the interiors designed by L. C. Tiffany & Associated Artists and its competitors of the period, a conscious attempt was made to decorate every visible surface.

tal fireplace with tiled-glass surround, surmounted by a stuccoed plaque depicting an epic battle between an eagle and a dragon; high oak wainscoting; decorative friezes (designed and executed for Tiffany by George H. Yewell and Frank D. Millet); and geometric stained-glass windows. The reaction of the critics was typical of what most of his room settings elicited: they thought it overdecorated and slightly too theatrical, but with individual parts that were often arresting in their originality.

Also in 1879, Tiffany and his family moved into the top floor of the Bella, an apartment house at 48 East Twenty-sixth Street, New York. This was the first of the four residences that he would own and inhabit, each of which came to exemplify his own distinctly personal mix of home and private art museum. Comprising a high, gabled interior, the apartment included several novel elements: a ceiling set with tiled-glass panels to supplement the light from the windows, bands of small inlays applied to the coffered ceiling in the lobby, and a stained-glass sash window operated by a wheel-and-pulley device that Tiffany chose to design and present as an ornamental object, rather than to conceal. There were built-in units to store and display objects—shelves, nooks, wall closets—throughout, all crammed with Oriental ceramics and metalwares. Several walls were painted India red or covered with blue Japanese textiles or Chinese matting. Above the mantel in the dining room hung a Tiffany painting of pumpkins, corn, and a turkey cock, rendered in yellow and red tones that complemented the glass light fixtures suspended throughout the apartment. A colorful and intimate, if perhaps somewhat congested, ambience prevailed, in which the artist had blended his love of the luxuriant and the exotic with current Victorian taste in furnishings.

A prestigious commission awaited the firm, one that underlined the astonishing speed with which it had achieved celebrity status within the world of interior design. In 1882, only three years after its inception, it received an invitation from President Chester Alan Arthur to refurbish parts of the White House, including several state rooms and the corridor separating the mansion's public and private sections. Arthur had been a wealthy New Yorker before ascending to the presidency, and is thought to have inspected the Seventh Regimental Armory and the Union League Club (on which L. C. Tiffany & Associated Artists had worked, together with Saint-Gaudens, La Farge, and Will H. Low) before settling on Tiffany for his decorating needs in the nation's capital.

Of special impact among the furnishings that Tiffany provided for the White House was a giant opalescent-glass screen, composed of three panels adorned along their perimeters with national emblems, that separated the main corridor from the vestibule leading into the family quarters. Also greatly admired was a series of mirrored wall sconces, fueled by gas jets, that created an impression of glittering, fragmented light. The bold optimism engendered by these alterations was relatively short-lived, however. Twenty-odd years later, Theodore Roosevelt again redecorated the mansion, this time choosing a Neoclassical style to evoke a mood of simple elegance, moderation, and charity. In doing so, he ordered Tiffany's glass screen removed. It was later destroyed.

How did Tiffany manage to enter the field of interior design with such apparent ease, and at such a rarefied social level? Neil Harris, in his insightful essay in *Masterworks of Louis Comfort Tiffany* (1989), provides an evaluation of the various elements of this complex question, and examines how they meshed to Tiffany's advantage. Of vital importance to his success was the changing attitude of the newly rich of the post–Civil War era; of their wish to enjoy their newfound wealth, and to do so unashamedly. The nation's earlier puritanism, which had manifested itself, in part, in the rejection of all forms of conspicuous consumption, yielded increasingly, from 1866 on, to the new generation's awareness of, and pride in, America's industrial might and spiraling prosperity. Why not celebrate, it was argued, and with jubilance? By the mid-1870s, many therefore openly indulged their appetite for an opulent life-style by the acquisition of art and antiques and—a necessary corollary—large mansions in which to house and display these trappings of financial success. As a visiting English critic, Cecilia Waern, noted in an 1897 article in *The Studio* that discussed America's delight in self-indulgence, "It would be almost absurd to expect a serious 'return to simplicity' in the land of mushroom fortunes." The mid-century ascetic imperatives of John Ruskin and, later, of Charles Eastlake were forgotten in the nation's rush to enjoy the profits of its mercantilism and entrepreneurship. A new flamboyance, exemplified for many Americans by illustrations of the Peacock Room, which Whistler designed for the residence of Francis R. Leyland in London in the mid-1870s, became the rallying cry for those who sought to enjoy and promote an elevated standard of living.

Tiffany's timing was clearly fortuitous: in the late 1870s and 1880s many of New York's wealthiest families were engaged in a genteel but earnest competition to construct spectacular residences, some of which were a full city block in length and rivaled in scale and splendor the palaces of Europe's aristocracy. Architectural and interior-design magazines, such as *Artistic Homes*, which was compiled and published in two volumes between 1882 and 1884 by George W. Sheldon, provided a visual document of how splendidly the rich and famous of the day lived. Publication of one's home and its interiors in such a review ensured enhanced status among one's peers, both for the homeowner and for the architect, decorator, and cabinet-maker who served as his interior designers.

Working closely with architects, particularly Stanford White, Tiffany had to persuade his clients that he could provide more provocative, and therefore more newsworthy, room settings than the rather formal and restrained eclecticism already offered by cabinetmakers such as Marcotté and Company, Pottier and Stymus, and Herter Brothers—all, by the late 1870s, well established in catering to the interior-decorating whims of the East Coast's millionaire set. Clearly, Tiffany would have to promote an entirely novel look to succeed against such proven competition.

In effect, three factors combined to propel Tiffany and his associates to the top rung of their new profession: his personal taste, the recommendations of the architects with whom he collaborated, and the prospective client's knowledge of, and respect for, his father's Fifth Avenue store. Of these, it was Tiffany's taste that forged the partnership's true identity. His strong affinity for Eastern cultures—his orientation, literally, to the arts of Persia, India, Byzantium, North Africa, and Japan—provided the artistic signature that quickly established the group in its clients' minds as fashionably different. To his love of the exotic Tiffany added a miscellany of typical Victorian decorative accents, including the liberal use of wainscoting, painted friezes, embroidered hangings, plush upholstery, tracer-

The hall in the Mark Twain residence, Hartford, Connecticut, which L. C. Tiffany & Associated Artists decorated in about 1882. The interior is to today's viewer practically indistinguishable from those created by most late Victorian interior design firms: there is a general eclecticism in the choice of furnishings, wall coverings, and accessories. Only Tiffany's use of glass in mosaic tiles and windows provides a key to its authorship.

A tiled mosaic mantelpiece in Tiffany's Seventy-second Street mansion, c. 1912. The row of Favrile glassware on the upper shelf probably included some of those pieces which he retained from the Studios' production for his own collection, and which were individually identified as "A. Coll." The inset shelves to the right of the hearth appear to house part of his collection of ancient glass.

ies, and his beloved glass tiles and transoms. The completed ensembles offered a blend of luxuriance, color, and illusion, in which the repeated use of certain images and materials provided stylistic continuity among commissions. Similar interiors, with minimum modifications, were installed in practically every type of urban structure: private homes, men's clubs, hotels, theaters, public institutions.

From the early 1880s on, Tiffany was busy with the preparation of a grand new residence, proposed by his father to house the entire family, that was built on the northwest corner of Madison Avenue at Seventy-second Street. The preliminary architectural designs were completed by Stanford White, with assistance from Tiffany, in a modern Romanesque style. Massive even by the scale of the mansions of other millionaires that lined Fifth and Park avenues, the building included an arched entrance fitted with an iron grill and porte cochère. For reasons not fully understood, Charles Lewis Tiffany did not move into the building, leaving his son and family to occupy the top two stories, which they did in 1885.

As in the Bella apartment, Tiffany filled the interior to excess with his favorite objects and furnishings, the informal marriage of Eastern and Western impulses reconfirming his unorthodox taste and talent as an interior decorator. Contemporary descriptions of the interior noted the masterful manipulation of space, light, and shadow, which was achieved in part through a combination of stained-glass windows, hanging glass globes, and an upper organ loft filled with vases of flowers and Oriental

PAINTING AND INTERIOR DESIGN

Drawing-room interior of the Hamilton Fish residence, 251 East Seventeenth Street, New York. L. C. Tiffany & Associated Artists remodeled the house in the early 1880s, when Fish was one of the country's leading elder statesmen. The interior work completed by Tiffany and his colleagues included the checkerboard wainscoting around the fireplace, the frame of the mantelpiece mirror, and the sections of beveled glass that border the central windowpane. They also designed some of the furniture, including the desk seen at lower left.

wares that reminded visitors of either *The Thousand and One Nights* or the palace of an Indian rajah. Of particular note in the top-floor studio was a central four-sided concrete fireplace, shaped like the bole of a tree, which cast a flickering glow on the conglomeration of Persian carpets, potted plants, furniture, and Indian and Japanese weapons, trophies, and mementos that spilled out to the room's perimeter.

Tiffany occupied the Seventy-second Street mansion until his death (he in fact died there). Objects were added and interchanged constantly as part of what he in 1916 termed his lifelong "quest for beauty." Charles de Kay attributed the interior's hodgepodge appearance in part to a certain spontaneity: "In some way or other Mr. Tiffany has filled the house with beautiful things and yet retained the home. How he has managed it is his own secret. Perhaps, like Topsy, 'It just growed.'"

L. C. Tiffany & Associated Artists remained in business for five years (1879–83), during which time the firm was commissioned not only by the American president, but by several of New York's most prominent and wealthy citizens. Included were Hamilton Fish, Henry De Forest (Lockwood's brother), J. Taylor Johnston (the founder of the Metropolitan Museum of Art), and Dr. William T. Lusk (who later became the Tiffany family's physician). Beyond Manhattan, the group decorated the castle of William S. Kimball, a Rochester industrialist, and the house of Samuel Clemens (Mark Twain) in Hartford, Connecticut. This last, like the Veterans Room in the Seventh Regimental Armory, has been restored

A drop-leaf desk (far left; detail, near left) commissioned for the William S. Kimball house in Rochester, New York. L. C. Tiffany & Associated Artists was employed to decorate the interior of the mansion in 1881. The desk, which appears to be similar to the one pictured in the Hamilton Fish house drawing room, was part of a four-piece satinwood library set that also included a writing table and two chairs. The furniture was probably designed by Lockwood De Forest, rather than by Tiffany himself.

largely to its original condition, providing the public with a further opportunity to view at first hand a typical Tiffany interior.

Despite the firm's obvious success, the individual artists became restless and eager to proceed with their own careers and interests, no doubt spurred in part by the fact that the fad for home decoration had begun to fade. As Candace Wheeler observed, "The wave of popular decorative art [had] broken over us and receded." The decision was therefore made in 1883 amicably to dissolve the partnership. Concerning Tiffany's own ambitions, Wheeler noted also, "I think Mr. Tiffany was rather glad to get rid

The parlor in the residence of J. Taylor Johnston, lower Fifth Avenue, New York, 1881–82, showing the familiar medley of styles provided by L. C. Tiffany & Associated Artists to its clients.

of us all, for his wonderful experiments in glass iridescence...meant far more to him at the time than association with other interests." In his memoirs, De Forest provided a similar account of the events, in mid-1882, leading to the firm's dissolution: "Soon after my return from India it became apparent that the organization of the Associated Artists as constituted would not work. A reorganization was important but we failed to agree as to how it should be done and broke up. Mrs. Wheeler took out all her department and I did mine with the India business. Mr. Tiffany and I divided the stock on hand."

Tiffany retained the premises at 333 Fourth Avenue, the others taking a studio at 115 East Twenty-third Street before themselves disbanding. Wheeler went on to design needlework and wallpapers for the Cheney Bros. and other commercial fabric houses, De Forest to spend more time in the Far East, and Colman to live in Newport, Rhode Island. The group's last collective enterprise was to decorate the interior of the Church of the Divine Paternity at Forty-fifth Street and Fifth Avenue, for which Wheeler designed embroideries, plush fabrics, and hangings.

The year 1884 provided a distressing interlude before Tiffany established his new firm, the Tiffany Glass Company. Steele MacKaye, for whom he and his associates had, as noted, decorated the Madison Square Theater in 1879, now invited Tiffany both to decorate his new theater, the Lyceum, and to participate in its financing. With John Cheney Platt and William Pringle Mitchell as junior partners, Tiffany contributed funds that he never recovered. The venture turned into a fiasco, requiring the financial intervention of Tiffany's father to stave off public embarrassment.

Earlier that year, personal disaster had struck when Tiffany's wife, Mary (May), died of tuberculosis. She had borne him three children (a fourth had died shortly after birth, while the family was traveling in France), and the marriage had been happy, despite the fact that she was continually plagued by frailty and ill health. She died on January 22, 1884, after an abortive attempt by the family's physician, William T. Lusk, to save her.

Tiffany's second wife, Louise Wakeman Knox, whom he married on November 9, 1886, came from the same social milieu as he. She was, in fact, his cousin once removed, and served as mother both to his surviving children—Mary (May-May), Charles Lewis, Jr., and Hilda—and, later, to the four daughters she bore him: the twins, Louise Comfort and Julia, Annie (who died at age four), and Dorothy.

Tiffany did not summarily cease, on the dissolution of L. C. Tiffany & Associated Artists, to offer his services as an interior designer and decorator. Both before and after the formation of the Tiffany Glass Company

View of the front facade of The Briars, Tiffany's first summer home, near Oyster Bay, New York, 1890s. Most of the family resisted the move to Laurelton Hall on its completion, in about 1904. They had grown to love The Briars, which they felt was a true home, unlike the monumental new mansion, which seemed rather to be a showpiece of Tiffany's wealth and self-esteem.

in 1885 he continued to accept commissions, including the New York residences of Ogden Goelet, Cornelius Vanderbilt II, and Henry Villard, and interiors for the Ponce de Leon Hotel that Bernard Maybeck designed for Henry Flagler in Saint Augustine, Florida. Later, in the early 1890s, he designed and furnished, for the Fifth Avenue mansion of Henry O. Havemeyer, a salon that in its unapologetic nonconformity was construed by the critics as a decorating disaster.

In 1890 Tiffany purchased a country estate near Oyster Bay, on the north shore of Long Island. Named The Briars, the house served as the family's summer home until the construction of Tiffany's final residence, Laurelton Hall, some fifteen years later. Tiffany remodeled the property's existing farmhouse through the years into a large shingled and shuttered dwelling with a central clock tower, surrounded by terraces, arbors, and landscaped gardens where he could paint and pursue his horticultural interests.

Also in the early 1890s, Tiffany began work on his most ambitious interior to date, the chapel that he exhibited at the 1893 Columbian Exposition in Chicago. The chapel, supplemented by exhibits called the Light and Dark Rooms, in which further fixtures of the company were displayed, was installed in space that had been reserved by his father's business, Tiffany & Company, in the Manufacturers and Liberal Arts Building. Variously described in the press as Byzantine or Romanesque, the interior was hailed as entirely original in concept: a sensory and kaleidoscopic tour de force in its application of colored glass to an ecclesiastical setting. Thousands thronged to feast their eyes on the orgy of glass mosaics and jewels, gilt metal, marble, mother-of-pearl, and semiprecious stones with which most of the liturgical objects in the chapel were embellished. Official recognition of the interior's impact was afforded by the award of fifty-four medals by the exposition jury.

Although the interior-design element of Tiffany's business yielded increasingly in the late 1880s to his preoccupation with glass and window making, Tiffany maintained it as an integral part of the multifaceted service that he offered to his clients. As late as 1913 a booklet published by Tiffany Studios, titled *Character and Individuality in Decorations and Furnishings*, listed the diversity of the firm's decorating services: period-revival interiors (especially in the Adam, Hepplewhite, and Queen Anne styles), rugs, metalware, glass, fabrics, upholstery, draperies, garden marbles, and furniture (the last-mentioned probably made to Tiffany's specifications by Schmitt Bros., a New York cabinetmaking firm). Illustrated were a host of rather stiff and nondescript room settings—none of which one would today readily associate with the artistic style that characterizes Tiffany's lamps and other household appliances and furnishings.

Preston Bradley Hall

A view of the library furnished by Tiffany Studios for the home of E. P. Sawyer in Oshkosh, Wisconsin, completed in 1908 (William Waters, architect). The Studios provided a mix of English and European period revival furnishings to complement Sawyer's antique furniture, in addition to a bronze entrance grill, a selection of glass lamps and chandeliers, and the arched wisteria window and doors leading from the library to the garden. The house is today the Oshkosh Public Museum.

Preston Bradley Hall in the Chicago Public Library Cultural Center, showing Tiffany's mosaic mural and giant glass dome, c. 1900.

Certificate of award, 1893 Columbian Exposition

WILLIAM WATERS, *Architect*   CORNER OF A LIVING ROOM   *Executed by* TIFFANY STVDIOS

THE WELL-APPOINTED HOME

is always regarded as an indubitable mark of taste and refinement. The TIFFANY STVDIOS have unusual facilities for planning and executing INTERIOR DECORATIONS, SPECIAL LIGHTING FIXTURES and FURNISHINGS and cordially invite an inspection of their DISTINCTIVE SERVICE, which consists of submitting colored sketches of a complete decorative scheme as well as samples of the HANGINGS, RUGS, FURNITURE and FIXTURES, so that one may see the effect produced and know the cost of same before any order is given or obligation incurred.

⊠ TIFFANY ⑤ STVDIOS ⊠
347-355 MADISON AVE.   COR.45TH ST.,NEW YORK CITY.
CHICAGO OFFICE,ORCHESTRA BVILDING – BOSTON OFFICE,LAWRENCE BVILDING.

A 1912 advertisement by Tiffany Studios, showing that even at this late date, when its reputation as the country's premier art-glass manufacturer was fully established, it continued to offer its clients a complete range of period-revival home furnishings.

A certificate of award from the 1893 Columbian Exposition in Chicago. The Tiffany Glass & Decorating Company was awarded fifty-four medals by the jury. The firm's display, a Byzantine chapel with two adjacent rooms decorated in part with examples of the firm's secular works, provided the public with its first full awareness of the scale and diversity of Tiffany's business.

Floral landscape window

II. The Windows and Mosaics

TIFFANY'S INVOLVEMENT IN THE MANUFACTURE of glass can be traced to the beginning of the 1870s, when he began to rent time at commercial glass furnaces in the New York area. The principal of these were the Heidt and Thill glasshouses in Brooklyn, where Tiffany and La Farge, among others, attempted to create a vibrant new range of colors in glass to supplement the small and dreary selection available commercially to local artists. Those glasshouses that specialized in the importation of English and European sheet glass for window production constituted, in the absence of a local glass-making industry, the only viable source of glass available to artists in the United States.

A booklet published by the company in the mid-1890s traces Tiffany's involvement to 1872, when "experiments in glass-making were instituted in New York, followed by valuable discoveries...which ultimately led to the invention of Tiffany Favrile glass." These seminal experiments, undertaken by Tiffany in a studio at the YMCA until an explosion occurred, were modest and limited primarily to the manufacture of molded-glass tiles and jewels that Tiffany applied as ornamental accents in his interiors. Initially in concert with La Farge—but soon in direct and often acrimonious competition with him—Tiffany pursued the creation of an opalescent variety of glass for use both as decorative trim and for window production.

La Farge and Tiffany were joined in their pursuit of a new glass by various other artist-designers, who banded together loosely to form the American School of Stained Glass as a professional association. Several characteristics identified the movement, particularly the use of opalescent sheet glass in which variegated colors were blended to provide an infinite range of tonal effects; the elimination of all painting and staining from windows, except where necessary to provide the flesh details in figural compositions; the use of plating (layering of more than one panel of glass) to achieve depths and nuances of color impossible in a single sheet; and the use of lead lines as an integral feature of design. The resulting style of window, generally called "pictorial," represented the renaissance claimed for it by its exponents, although critics denounced it for its resemblance to the dissimilar field of painting on canvas, in which the image was seen by reflected, rather than transmitted, light.

Floral landscape window

c. 1912. Leaded Favrile glass, 57 x 38"
Signed lower right, TIFFANY STUDIOS
NEW YORK
Private collection

A contemporary article on this commission noted that the window comprised three kinds of flowers—sweet peas, daisies, and carnations—that no artist had been able previously to define in glass without using hand painting.

5 1

Cartoon for a figural window

Tiffany's experimentations in glass proceeded slowly, and no doubt unevenly, throughout the 1870s, his progress hampered by the fact that he was dependent on others—the commercial glasshouses and their staffs—for kiln time and chemical glass-making expertise. The fact that competitors had equal access to the same facilities probably also restrained him from a headlong pursuit of radical techniques and formulae whose secrecy he could not ensure. He was therefore at the time very much on an equal footing with his competitors; all were restricted to the same selection of materials and production facilities. The development of his inimitable Favrile glass, which became the proud imprimatur of his mature works, was many years away.

Windows

Around 1876 Tiffany won his first window commission, a lunette for the Church of the Sacred Heart on West Fifty-first Street in New York. His design was composed of a series of bull's-eyes (small roundels of glass) placed in graduating rows; to today's viewer it appears remarkably uninspired, even taking account of the fact that this marked his debut as a window designer. Two years later he provided a figural window for Saint Mark's Episcopal Church in Islip, New York, on Long Island's south shore, comprising a painted figure of the apostle seated against a background of roundels that simulated a central nimbus within a bank of circular clouds. Again the composition is nondescript, completely lacking in features that would identify it as the work of Tiffany, as distinct from one of his competitors. Clearly, at this point, the family name provided a necessary cachet in Tiffany's pursuit of window commissions; he had yet to establish himself in his own right as a glass artist.

The late 1870s also brought the first of Tiffany's commissions for domestic windows. These he executed both for wealthy private clients and for his own residences. Noteworthy among them were two overdoor transoms that he executed in 1879 for the home of George Kemp. Designed as matching panels of trellised squash and eggplants, the two have survived to provide an invaluable record of Tiffany's earliest designs as a glass artist and to reveal the range of colors and textures in glass then available to him. Although the two compositions today appear somewhat stiff and tentative, and therefore uncharacteristic of Tiffany's later works, they were rendered entirely without paint, which was revolutionary for the period.

Around this time Tiffany designed several windows for himself, including a curious, yet progressive, abstract panel that he installed in his home in the Bella Apartments. His appointment, around 1878, of an

Cartoon for an ecclesiastical window, probably designed by Frederick Wilson

c. 1900. Watercolor on board, 7¾ x 6¾"
Unsigned, inscribed lower left, 5x95
Private collection

Characteristic of the thousands of church windows completed during the firm's nearly fifty years in existence, this cartoon portrays a scene that met, in its iconography, what most churches expected in a religious memorial window: a depiction of an event in the Scriptures with which the congregation could easily identify.

Italian, Andrea Boldini, to manage his glasshouse operations, marked a further step on his road to independence as a glass manufacturer.

By the end of the 1870s, although he still did not have his own furnaces, Tiffany could boast various technical glass-making innovations, particularly those used in the manufacture of ornamental tiles. These he combined in three patent applications filed on October 25, 1880; the patents were granted the following February. Mostly square in form and with relief patterns such as rosettes or dragons, the tiles were molded in a single operation from pot-metal glass of various monochromatic colors for application in domestic and ecclesiastical settings.

A notable surviving example of this type of Tiffany tilework is the fireplace surround in the Veterans Room in the Seventh Regimental Armory, installed in 1880. Molded-glass globes, for incorporation in the light fixtures that he designed for interiors such as this one and the Havemeyer residence on Fifth Avenue, provided Tiffany with a further application for his invention.

Cartoon for a figural window designed by Frederick Wilson

c. 1900.
Watercolor on board, 13 x 3¾"
Signed lower right and inscribed, top, *DECEMBER 11*
Private collection

Frederick Wilson was the most gifted and longest-serving of the window designers at Tiffany Studios. Over nearly thirty years, he designed thousands of religious figural windows and mosaics, most of which were memorials for church or mausoleum settings. He left Tiffany in the early 1920s, establishing his own design studio in southern California. This unidentified cartoon appears to celebrate a wedding ceremony.

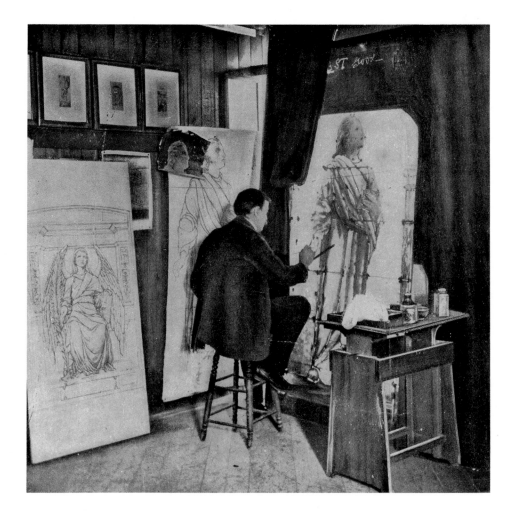

An artist at the Tiffany Glass & Decorating Company, c. 1899, paints the facial and hand features onto the figure of Christ in a memorial window. No further painted detailing was permitted on most windows produced at the Studios. Indeed, Tiffany was fiercely proud that all other decorative elements in his windows could be achieved in the glass itself, without the application of the industry's traditional enamel-based paints or stains, which were largely opaque and therefore interrupted the transmission of light through glass.

Tiffany's progress in his adopted medium accelerated in the 1880s at a pace that appears to have been related directly to his growing disenchantment with the profession of interior design. The field, at the time, was neither so fashionable nor so prestigious as it is today, supported by the haut monde and featured in the glossy magazines that now document prevailing tastes. Impatient for individual success, he searched increasingly within the world of stained glass for the recognition that he felt had eluded him as an interior decorator. It was to this end that the partnership of Tiffany & Associated Artists was amicably dissolved in 1883.

On December 1, 1885, Tiffany embarked formally on his new venture with the formation of his new firm, the Tiffany Glass Company. He was finally on the road to an independent career in the applied arts, one that would bring him international acclaim perhaps even beyond his own considerable ambitions. No doubt his second marriage, in 1886, helped to focus him on his new goals after a period of disorientation that had worried his family, and particularly his father, in the preceding years.

Tiffany was preoccupied increasingly in the 1880s with administrative matters as he strove to meet the explosion of church-construction

Tiffany's window department, about 1899, showing several windows in assembly. The system for manufacturing stained-glass windows has remained basically unchanged since the Middle Ages: individual pieces of glass are held in place with lead cames that are secured at their joints with solder. The gas soldering irons evident in this photograph have, however, during the last twenty years, largely been replaced within the industry by electric ones.

A worker applies extra panels of glass to the back or front of a Tiffany window, a last stage in balancing the color harmony before completing a commission. In this process, the window was placed against the light and examined to see if certain areas of color were too bright, or of the wrong hue, within the overall composition. In certain instances, seven or eight layers have been found on Tiffany windows, evidence of the Studios' assiduous search for perfection.

Cartoon for an allegorical window depicting "Power," designed by Frederick Wilson

1900. Watercolor and pencil on paper, 10 x 7″
Unsigned
Collection of Mary C. Higgins, Camden, Maine

Nonreligious figural themes such as this were often commissioned by university libraries, private men's clubs, and other institutions.

activity that followed the Civil War. The nation was experiencing a fervid spiritual resurgence that led to a demand for numerous new church buildings. In 1875 alone, over four thousand churches of all denominations were under construction, each to be proudly embellished with memorials to cherished former communicants and members of the clergy. Tiffany found himself perfectly placed to capitalize on the increased demand for stained-glass commissions.

The tempo of church construction continued throughout the decade, drawing Tiffany increasingly away from his role as artist-designer into that of entrepreneur. To offset this shift in his responsibilities, he began in the mid-1880s to assemble the team of designers who formed the nucleus of the window department of his company, and remained so well into the new century. The decision was clearly advantageous, freeing him from the need personally to design religious figural windows, which represented by far the majority of church-window commissions at the time. Not only was Tiffany weak in drawing the human form, but he also lacked formal training in biblical iconography, both prerequisites for a designer of church memorials. By releasing these commissions to his professional window designers, and retaining for himself only those for prized clients, Tiffany effectively balanced his time between artistic and commercial considerations. To maintain final control of the firm's production, however, he initiated a system whereby all of the designs prepared by the window department were reviewed by him before they were submitted to customers. The firm's surviving window cartoons invariably bear Tiffany's penciled initials under the heading *Approved By*, often with extensive notations by him in the margins, and later press releases were careful to reiterate the fact that Tiffany was ultimately responsible for all work, their opening sentences always announcing a newly completed commission as "under the supervision of Louis Comfort Tiffany."

By the middle of the 1880s, the secular windows Tiffany designed for private clients and for his own needs had increased noticeably in both number and aesthetic importance. An 1885 commission for Mary Elizabeth Garrett of Baltimore, in particular, showed the growing power of his sensitivities as a colorist and naturalist in glass. Its design of flowers, fishbowls, fruit, and scrolled ribbons anticipated some of his most successful floral windows of the early 1900s in a compact and vigorous composition that allowed the introduction of a kaleidoscope of delicately blended colors. Another highly appealing work, datable roughly to the same year, was the five-panel magnolia and wisteria window he installed in the Tiffany mansion on Seventy-second Street, New York. Set against a background of clear glass, the flowers appear to be growing against the exterior of the window, a clever bit of trompe l'oeil that drew the view

THE WINDOWS AND MOSAICS

beyond the house into the room. Examination of the surviving sections of the window (now in the Morse Museum of American Art, Winter Park, Florida) reveals one of the technical innovations that Tiffany introduced intermittently into his adopted medium: the lead cames are realistically milled and sculpted to simulate real magnolia branches.

The firm's design department was formed from members of the craft's itinerant labor force, which by tradition circulated among local glasshouses as business necessitated. Foremost among these was Joseph Lauber (1855–1948), a German immigrant who had worked previously for John La Farge, and who remained with Tiffany from 1888 to 1892. Lauber was a gifted and versatile artist who switched easily between the disciplines of window and mosaic design, sculpture, and mural painting. Other early recruits were Will H. Low (1853–1932), another gifted mixed-medium artist and craftsman, and Jacob Adolphus Holzer (1858–1938), a Swiss-born muralist, mosaicist, interior designer, and sculptor who had been associated previously with both La Farge and Saint-Gaudens. Clearly, these designers brought invaluable experience and technical expertise—particularly for liturgical commissions—to the Tiffany Glass Company in its formative years, as did others slightly later, such as Edward Peck Sperry (d. 1925) and Frederick Wilson (1858–1932), who succeeded Holzer as the chief designer of the window department in 1897. A portraitist and cartoonist armed with an inexhaustible knowledge of Old and New Testament iconography, Wilson emerged as the firm's most prolific and talented designer of figural windows and mosaic friezes, producing the bulk of its church memorials until his departure in 1923.

In a discussion of Tiffany's principal designers, mention must also be made of Agnes J. Northrop, who joined the women's work force in the glass department in 1884, at age twenty-seven, and who was promoted later to the window department. Northrop became the principal designer after Tiffany of nonfigural landscape and floral window compositions. So similar was her style to his that today it is impossible in many instances, without documentation, to attribute designs to one or the other with certainty. In 1933, when the firm closed, Northrop joined those employees who established the Westminster Memorial Studios in New York to complete Tiffany's outstanding commissions. She retired in 1936.

Through the years, Tiffany invited independent artists to contribute designs for windows, while some also were retained by the families or institutions who initiated commissions. The most eminent of these were Frederick Stuart Church, Howard Pyle, Lydia Field Emmett, Maxfield Parrish, and Frank Brangwyn. As a pragmatic businessman, Tiffany was unconcerned that the participation of such artists might diminish in the

Christ Blessing Children, cartoon for a memorial window

c. 1900. Wash and pencil on paper, 10 x 8"
Unsigned
Collection of Edward Hewett,
Vineyard Haven, Massachusetts

The theme was frequently used to memorialize the death of a child. To ensure its bold claim that none of its commissions were ever identical, the design department of the Studios often introduced subtle, if not indiscernible, variations in its designs for windows based on the same theme. The fact that these were often placed in churches far apart and of different denominations helped the firm to conceal from clients the fact that it did on occasion resort to earlier, proven designs for new commissions.

Angel of the Resurrection, President Benjamin Harrison Memorial window

public's eye his role in a window's creation. The completed commission was made of glass, a medium that was clearly in his domain. Indeed, his firm could only gain status from such associations. Similarly, he permitted his designers to translate into glass the masterworks of old-master and nineteenth-century painters. Included were works by Sandro Botticelli, Raphael, Annibale Carracci, Gustave Doré, William Holman Hunt, and—a perennial favorite in the firm's early years—the German artist

Feeding the Flamingoes

Before 1893. Watercolor on paper
Unsigned
Location unknown

This painting became the cartoon for one of the two secular windows Tiffany exhibited at the 1893 Columbian Exposition, in a room adjacent to his Byzantine chapel (the window and a second version of this painting are in the collection of the Morse Museum of American Art, Winter Park, Florida).

Heinrich Hoffmann. The majority of these were biblical scenes and were for placement in churches and mausoleums. Despite the firm's proud claim through the years that it never duplicated its window designs—that each was created for a specific client and never repeated—several of these masterpiece paintings were reproduced in windows that Tiffany was careful to place in churches of differing denominations, often thousands of miles apart.

By the end of the 1880s, the Tiffany Glass Company was firmly established as the largest stained-glass studio in the nation, its success due almost entirely to the continuing boom in church construction. Commissions ranged from single memorial windows to entire interiors, for which the firm designed and executed all of the liturgical accessories, including marble altars and retables, oak pews, mosaic plaques and friezes, and bronze chandeliers and candelabra. If content with his entrepreneurial accomplishments, however, Tiffany remained unfulfilled as an artist. His principal client, the church, insisted on an endless repertoire of traditional religious figural windows, which denied him the opportunity to incorporate in his designs the renderings of nature—both panoramas and floral studies—for which he had distinguished himself as a painter. The market for domestic windows remained relatively small and sporadic, and could certainly not sustain him professionally. Tiffany's visit to the 1889 Exposition Universelle Internationale in Paris brought a further frustration. On view was a floral window by his arch-competitor, La Farge, that the critics hailed as a masterpiece. Tiffany sought out Siegfried Bing (generally known as S. Bing), who ran an art gallery in the French capital and from whom he had purchased Oriental works, and advised him that he himself was about to create an important secular window. The meeting was auspicious, helping Tiffany to win Bing's allegiance in the coming years, which for both would prove momentous.

The history of Tiffany as a master glassmaker and artist really begins in 1892, with the establishment of his own glass furnaces in Corona, New York. That same year he changed the name of his firm to the Tiffany Glass & Decorating Company. Now, finally, he could pursue his experimentation in private and with his own staff of chemists and gaffers, some of whom were lured from the glass-making center of Stourbridge, England. Contemporary accounts noted the frenzied activity of the furnaces from their inception, in part in preparation for an important coming event—the Columbian Exposition in Chicago—in which Tiffany was to make his international debut.

The 1893 Columbian Exposition catapulted Tiffany to national recognition. His exhibit, comprising primarily a lavishly gilded and ornate Byzantine chapel, drew hordes of visitors and accolades from the critics.

The adjacent Dark and Light Rooms were less spectacular, but held the key to his imminent break with traditional conformity in their presentation of a selection of secular windows. One of these in particular, depicting parakeets perched among fruit blossoms and peering into a hanging goldfish bowl, captivated viewers with its charming choice of subject matter and delicate naturalist palette. Most of the public had never had access to the homes of the wealthy who commissioned windows with nonreligious themes, and now saw for the first time that stained-glass windows did not have to be religiously inspired; they could also have artistic value in other settings.

Buoyed by his reception at the exposition, Tiffany set out to conquer the international market, passing La Farge on his way up as the latter, dogged increasingly by the financial crises that punctuated his career, fell into decline. With the assistance of Bing, by now his most ardent publicist, Tiffany exhibited in 1895 in Paris at both the Salon du Champs-de-Mars (the salon of the Société Nationale des Beaux-Arts) and Bing's gallery L'Art Nouveau. In New York he produced a series of windows designed

Vase of Red Peonies window

c. 1900–1905. Leaded Favrile glass. 56 x 39"
Unsigned
Private collection

This window was commissioned by James B. Castle for his residence in Waikiki, Hawaii. Another version exists, depicting a similar vase of red peony blossoms, but including pieces of glass and glazing techniques that suggest that it was executed some years earlier. The density of color achieved by Tiffany in his glass—evident, particularly, in the red and blue hues in this composition—allowed him to create studies of nature that transcended reality in their intensity.

for Bing by Pierre Bonnard, Edouard Vuillard, and other members of the Nabis. The critics were mixed in their reviews, one, Léon de Fourcand, referring to the Nabis' windows as "ce bizarre manifeste" in *La Revue des arts décoratifs*. Clearly, Bing's "new art" was still too new, although Tiffany could claim by association to be linked to the world of avant-garde French painting.

Another important international forum was the exhibition Bing held at the Grafton Galleries in London in 1899. Of Bing's commissioned art-

Landscape window with peacock, commissioned by Mrs. E. F. Leary for the staircase of her Seattle home

c. 1908. Leaded Favrile glass, 192 x 90″
Signed lower right, *TIFFANY STUDIOS NEW YORK*
The Thomas Burke Memorial Washington State
Museum, University of Washington, Seattle

In many landscape windows such as this, it remains unclear whether Tiffany himself or one of his staff created the initial design. Many landscape and floral windows were designed by Agnes Northrop, who joined the firm in the 1880s, and whose artistic style was very similar to that of Tiffany. Like Tiffany, Northrop specialized in nonfigural compositions of flowers and landscapes. Surviving records indicate that in many instances Northrop prepared the preliminary sketches for Tiffany's approval, and, after his changes had been incorporated, redrafted a finished window cartoon.

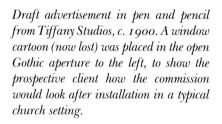

Draft advertisement in pen and pencil from Tiffany Studios, c. 1900. A window cartoon (now lost) was placed in the open Gothic aperture to the left, to show the prospective client how the commission would look after installation in a typical church setting.

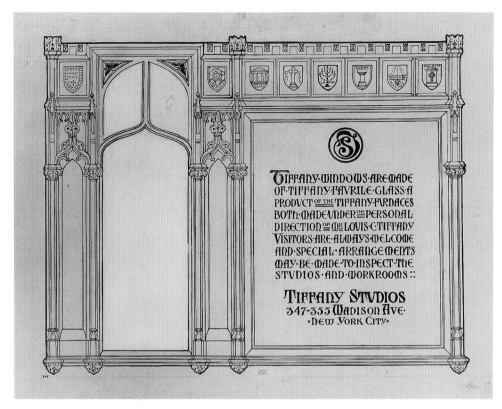

ists, Tiffany was the most comprehensively represented. As the critic Horace Townsend noted in *The Studio* that year: "Never before has so extensive an exhibit as this been made, Mr. Tiffany having stripped his studios and stores bare in order to more fully and thoroughly represent himself in English eyes." The windows, interspaced with cabinets of his blown art glass, were awash with color, presenting a stark challenge to the mediocrity of English stained glass from the heart of the enemy camp. The exhibition catalogue revealed that most of these windows were secular; those with religious themes were represented where possible by cartoons, rather than by the windows themselves. After these exhibitions, Tiffany reviewed carefully what he felt would best represent him at the coming 1900 Exposition Universelle in Paris, an event of incomparable importance if he wished to win the respect of the international art community. Clearly, this would expose him to a constituency completely different from that of the church, his prime customer at home, and one that as an artist he coveted far more.

On the threshold of the new century, Tiffany could observe his progress with deep satisfaction. He had, after nearly three long decades, perfected the glass-making process so that the inventory of window glass at the Corona works included over five thousand colors and textures, all carefully coded and filed for easy identification. There was, quite simply, no effect or mood in glass that his staff could not achieve, either in a single sheet, or in layered combinations. Now over fifty years of age, he had finally mastered his medium and could reap its rewards. He had even, shortly before 1900, persuaded a handful of ministers to allow him to install in their churches windows depicting landscapes or floral compositions in preference to traditional biblical scenes. To counter the predictable criticism that such a fundamental change would generate, the firm issued press releases that linked the naturalistic themes directly to the Creator. The windows, they argued, were an attempt to draw on "the endless wealth of precept and suggestion that lies around us in air and water and earth, in all the vast teeming bosom of Nature." Far from being sacrilegious, the floral theme was in fact pantheistic, drawing its inspiration directly from God's work.

The 1900 Exposition Universelle set the capstone on Tiffany's career. His exhibit in the American pavilion, alongside that of his father's firm, Tiffany & Company, won him awards in several categories. While raving about his art glass, however, the critics were guarded in their praise of his windows, particularly those that were ecclesiastical in theme. One window in particular, called *The Flight of Souls*, represented for several critics the unresolved problems of Tiffany's artistry. Herwin Schaefer's later review of the window was typical of the ambivalence it engendered: "Even now," he wrote,

at the height of his fame, the beauty and richness of the glass did not blind the critics to the frequent inadequacy of Tiffany's designs, an inadequacy which was basically one of misusing his decorative material for pictorial purposes. When he created a window entitled "The Flight of the Soul" [sic]... one understands the critic who called it froid, triste, obscur *even though it was made of Tiffany's justly famous glass. However, the lower part of this window was taken up by bushes of flowers which actually served merely as a pretext to introduce elements of color, and this part of the window shows Tiffany to much better advantage because he does not try to serve ideas or sentiment but lets the magic of his material speak in its own right.*

The floral windows that Tiffany exhibited at the exposition, such as *The Four Seasons* and a panel depicting snowball bushes in blossom, reinforced the belief within the art community that his aesthetic strength lay in the glorious color of his glass and not in his attempt to portray pictorial events. If nothing else, Tiffany was reminded that his two constituencies—that for ecclesiastical and that for domestic windows—should be kept well apart if he was to maintain their respective loyalties.

Having achieved both celebrity and a satisfying level of artistic quality in 1900, Tiffany was now inundated with new commissions, and never

Landscape panel (detail)

c. 1910. Leaded Favrile glass, 30 x 45″
Unsigned
Collection of Colonel and Mrs. Jake Rudd,
New Jersey

This panel is typical of the numerous domestic commissions executed by the Studios through the years for private clients. Most, like this, were unsigned, for the reason that Tiffany considered each a unique work designed for a specific client, which therefore required no further identification. The fact that such private commissions, for reasons of client confidentiality, were excluded from the interim lists of completed window commissions published by the Tiffany Studios complicates the research done today by historians to determine their provenance.

again felt the need to present such a comprehensive array of his works at exhibition. In 1900 he once again changed the company's name, to Tiffany Studios, and incorporated several autonomous divisions into the firm, including glass furnaces and a metal foundry. At the Pan-American Exposition the following year in Buffalo, New York, records indicate, the firm displayed several of the windows shown in Paris and designs for others; but in general his displays in international expositions after the turn of the century emphasized household items, especially Favrile glassware and enamels, and sometimes lamps. Rather, he turned his attention to his ongoing campaign to persuade church traditionalists to accept his unorthodox window imagery. As earlier resistance began to erode, he was able to place landscape and floral panels here and there in churches of all denominations across the country.

If he did not exhibit many windows, Tiffany nevertheless now began a spectacular period of ecclesiastical and secular window production, and work after work of breathtaking beauty and technical complexity now

THE WINDOWS AND MOSAICS

Angels of Praise, cartoon for a memorial window

Undated. Watercolor and pencil on paper,
20½ x 11″
Unsigned
The Metropolitan Museum of Art, New York.
The Elisha Whittelsey Collection,
the Elisha Whittelsey Fund, 1953

Commissioned by Frederic C. D. Urant of Philadelphia, this cartoon adopts the mosaic, or brickwork, pattern characteristic of the medallion windows of the Middle Ages, when glassmakers could make glass only in tiny sheets or fragments. This, in turn, made it necessary for the window designers of the era to divide their compositions into very small sections of glass.

WHEREFORE BY THEIR FRUITS YE SHALL KNOW THEM.
ST. MAT. VII-20
IN LOVING RECOGNITION OF THE GOOD WORKS OF JOHN AND TERRESSA DANNER
BE THOU FAITHFUL UNTO DEATH, AND I WILL GIVE THEE A CROWN OF LIFE.
REV. II-10

The Danner Memorial window

The Clara A. Greer Memorial window

The Clara A. Greer Memorial window

1914. Leaded Favrile glass, 96 x 42″
Unsigned
Christ Episcopal Church, Rye, New York

The Studios produced a range of ecclesiastical windows inspired by the medallion windows found in Gothic cathedrals such as those at Chartres and Reims.

The Danner Memorial window

1913. Leaded Favrile glass, 192 x 128″
Signed and dated lower right, TIFFANY STUDIOS
NEW YORK 1913
Private collection, Japan

Commissioned by the family of John and Terressa Danner in honor of their parents for the First Baptist Church, Canton, Ohio. The Danners owned a successful local coachmaking business and were typical of the prosperous church-going families in small regional towns who found it fashionable to commission Tiffany Studios for their family memorial. This beautiful window represents the work of the Tiffany Studios at its pinnacle, not only in its monumental size, but in the inclusion of a wide selection of the finest Favrile glass.

Landscape window

c. 1912–15. Leaded Favrile glass, 60 x 48″
Unsigned
Private collection

The careful selection of glass throughout the window, including that of the graining on the wooden fence, the rippled texture of the water, and the cloud formations in the sky, permitted the Tiffany Studios to achieve the most naturalistic effects in glass in the history of the medium. The piece was originally executed for a mansion at 73 Hemenway Street, the Fenway, Boston.

Eight-panel autumnal landscape window

c. 1915. Leaded Favrile glass, 66 x 116″
Signed lower right
Private collection

This spectacular window captures the dramatic red, orange, and yellow palette of the North American fall and, in the addition of deep blues and purples, creates a highly romantic effect. The cartoon for the window is in the collection of the Morse Museum of American Art, Winter Park, Florida. The window was commissioned by P. B. Griffin for the stair landing of his mansion in Jersey City, New Jersey.

came onto the market. Many of his most exceptional creations—such as those for Mrs. E. F. Leary (1908), the Danner Memorial window for the First Baptist Church of Canton, Ohio (1913), *The Bathers,* intended for display at the 1915 Panama-Pacific Exposition in San Francisco, and an eight-panel autumn landscape scene commissioned by P. B. Griffin of Jersey City (c. 1915)—were executed between this time and 1915. The window department, which at times numbered as many as two hundred designers and artisans, could generate an astonishing volume of commissions with apparent ease. Unfortunately, no official record appears to have survived of many of the commissions undertaken after 1910, the year the firm published the last of its three lists of completed commissions (1893, 1897, and 1910; the last two updated).

Eight-panel autumnal landscape window

Cartoon for a landscape window

1923. Watercolor over black ink and graphite
on paper, 11⅞ x 8⅜"
Unsigned
The Metropolitan Museum of Art, New York.
Transferred from archives, 1958. 58–658

Surviving Tiffany Studios literature lists this as the last window project in which Tiffany actively participated. Commissioned by Mr. L. D. Towle for his residence in Boston, and donated in 1925 to the Metropolitan Museum of Art, New York, the window is now on permanent display in the sculpture garden of the museum's American Wing.

After 1915 the artistic level of the firm's windows declined as the earlier spate of church building slowed, and as Tiffany himself withdrew gradually from day-to-day operations. Approaching seventy years of age, he occupied himself increasingly with the establishment of a personal legacy, which formally came into being in 1918 with the creation of the Louis Comfort Tiffany Foundation. He did, though, apply himself to window design on occasion, in the early 1920s, for example, supervising for a Mr. L. D. Towle of Boston the design of the landscape window now installed in the American Wing of the Metropolitan Museum of Art, New York.

THE WINDOWS AND MOSAICS

Cartoon for the Charles Duncan and William G. Hegardt Memorial window, Pilgrim Congregational Church, Duluth, Minnesota

c. 1924. Watercolor on paper, 5⅞ x 5″
Unsigned
Private collection

By the time this window was commissioned, in the mid-1920s, Tiffany had eliminated practically all resistance among church bodies to his introduction of landscape or floral windows such as this into ecclesiastical settings.

The window department continued to execute numerous commissions throughout the twenties and early thirties under the guidance of, among others, Agnes Northrop. Although many orders completed during this period were clearly adapted from earlier ones, it is the precipitous decline in workmanship and quality of glass that distinguishes most of these windows from earlier works.

Mosaics

Largely ignored in studies of Tiffany's achievements in glass have been the new dimensions that he brought to the field of mosaicwork. The medium, which can trace its heritage to the frescoes and tiled courtyards of imperial Rome, Pompeii, Byzantium, and Ravenna, is traditionally a composition broken down into a matrix composed of small squares of glass,

Interior, Chapel of Our Lady, Cathedral of Saint Louis

Te Deum Laudamus, mosaic mural triptych

1922–23. Favrile glass mosaic, three panels, each 204 x 96″
The Lake Park United Methodist Church, Oakland, California

Designed by Frederick Wilson for the First United Methodist Church, Los Angeles, the mural depicts, left, Saint Paul in a procession of choristers; center, Christ seated in glory, attended by angels; and right, Saint John reading from the Holy Book, accompanied by a procession of thurifers. Removed some years ago from its original setting, the triptych is now in storage in Oakland, California.

Interior, Chapel of Our Lady, Cathedral of Saint Louis, Saint Louis, Missouri, c. 1912

Tiffany's largest mosaic commission was the interior of the Roman Catholic cathedral in Saint Louis. Working to designs created by Chevalier Aristedes Leonori, architect to the pope, a team of Tiffany Studios mosaicists installed 30 million glass tesserae in the cathedral at a cost of roughly $2 million. This is a contemporary photograph from the Tiffany Studios files. No doubt at the Vatican's insistence, the Studios adhered to the traditional Italian checkerboard method of mosaic application in its execution of the commission.

Mosaic wall mirror

Mosaic plaque

c. 1900. Favrile glass mosaic, 13⅜ x 13½″
Unsigned
The Corning Museum of Glass, Corning,
New York

Mosaic wall mirror

c. 1900–1905. Favrile glass mosaic with
bronze frame, 32 x 24″
Signed, on reverse of bronze frame,
TIFFANY STUDIOS, NEW YORK
Private collection

*This was apparently a unique commission
for a wealthy client; the artistic quality of
the design and its high level of workmanship make one regret that Tiffany did not
undertake more domestic commissions of
this caliber. Viewed from an angle, the
high iridescence of the frame's surface
makes it appear radiant, or internally lit.*

*Small mosaics such as this were designed
to serve as stands and trivets for toiletry
items, or to be inset into marble friezes in
architectural settings. The Studios employed young women rather than men to
complete its mosaic commissions, thinking
them more dextrous in working with small
glass tesserae. They were paid a lower
rate, and this threatened the male staff,
who on several occasions went on strike in
protest. The issue was partially resolved
(in the men's opinion, at least) when it
was noted that the young women often got
married and left to have children. Eventually the staffs were mixed.*

called tesserae, interspersed with a few *sectiliae,* or pieces cut into irregular shapes. As such, it has proved a colorful and durable medium, impervious to practically all damage except fire.

As in his windows, Tiffany was at first forced by his primary client, the church, and institutions such as libraries and universities, to conform to the classical mosaic style, even though the original reason for its compact checkerboard form of assembly—that glass in the pre-Christian era could be blown or cast only in very small pieces—had long since ceased to be a design constraint. The church's rigid traditionalism, however, obliged Tiffany to provide a conventional interpretation in all of his ecclesiastical commissions, not only for mosaic panels and friezes, but for all liturgical objects, such as baptismal fonts, altars, retables, and lecterns, which he enriched with decorative glass inlays. These works were composed of infinitesimal pieces of glass painstakingly cut and assembled by the firm's team of mosaicists, which between 1898 and 1913 grew from twelve to fifty-six in number; much of the craftsmanship, however, was perfunctory. Most of the team's completed commissions, in fact, warrant respect as much for their monumental scale as for their artistry. The Roman Catholic cathedral in Saint Louis, for example, built in 1912, included five hundred mosaic panels designed by the pope's architect, Chevalier Aristedes Lenori, comprising 30 million pieces of glass. No doubt profitable and prestigious for Tiffany, the commission represented something for the record books rather than an artistic achievement. It is still intact. Other large mosaic works, such as those for the Alexander Commencement Hall at Princeton University, Saint Mark's English Lutheran Church in Baltimore, the Chicago Public Library, and, most notably, Tiffany's first public exhibition of his mosaics, the Byzantine chapel at the 1893 Columbian Exposition, were bright and spectacular, and always of an irreproachable technical excellence, but all were based on the gridlike tesseraic format of antiquity. Even Tiffany's vibrant glass could not free these compositions from their classical stiffness and monochromatic look. In short, like his church windows, they lacked originality. Similarly, the firm's early nonreligious figural mosaic compositions, such as a frieze illustrating the crossing of the Northwest Passage, designed by Holzer for the Marquette Building in Chicago (still in situ), were often flat and motionless.

In concert with his attempt to liberate himself from the church's stranglehold on ecclesiastical window design, Tiffany began, toward 1900, to impose his own style on commissions for secular mosaics. These, for the most part, were decorative panels set in bronze mounts that were intended to be hung on the wall like paintings. Eliminated was the classical grid format; in its place, he used irregular pieces of glass of unrestricted and variable size; this enabled him to pursue the same realistic effects, including those of shadowing and perspective, that he sought in his windows. His compositions for mosaics and windows, in fact, now became identical, with the sharp distinction only that the two mediums were diametrically opposed in concept: the one was to be viewed by a reflected light, the other by a transmitted one.

The unlimited palette of Tiffany's glass, with its vibrant surface iridescence, on which the changing light generated myriad nuances of tone and hue, completed his rejuvenation of the medium. The selection of his glass for peacock plumage and the glittering scales of fish, for example, far exceeded reality in its lustered brilliance. To enhance this effect, sections of bright metallic foil were placed beneath the mosaics to intensify their reflective qualities in those instances where the glass was not fully opalescent and therefore absorbed some light rays.

Unfortunately, it appears from the firm's literature that Tiffany was afforded relatively few opportunities to develop this form of mosaic decoration, beyond a handful of large commissions. These included the *Dream Garden* mural for the foyer of the Curtis Publishing Company building in Philadelphia (still in place), the fountain mural now installed in the sculpture garden in the American Wing at the Metropolitan Museum of Art, New York, and the still-extant proscenium curtain in the National Theater in Mexico City. Birds, fish, and flowers proved ideal themes for domestic panels, but these were less popular when executed in mosaics than in window form.

Tiffany's use of mosaics within the home was extended also to the application of tesserae to bronze table-lamp bases and desk-top items such as paperweights, inkstands, and candlesticks, for which they served as lavish color accents. It was in his decorative panels, however, that Tiffany developed their fullest artistic expression.

Mosaic panel with two parrots in exotic foliage

c. 1905. Favrile glass mosaic, 44 (height of wooden frame) x 10¼"
Unsigned
Private collection

In contrast to the medium's conventional checkerboard technique of execution, the shapes of the tesserae here follow the natural outlines of the objects in the composition. This was one of Tiffany's major contributions to the modern mosaicist's art: that he freed it from its traditional grid form and static look.

Fish Cameo vase

III. *The Industrial Arts*

THE ESTABLISHMENT OF THE GLASS FURNACES at Corona in 1893 effectively launched Tiffany on a secondary career, one through which he could pursue the domestic American market directly. Until that time he had worked largely for a single client, the church, in the creation of a comprehensive range of liturgical items. Whereas many of these commissions (especially memorial windows) had been for individual members of a congregation, and therefore for the public at large, the church remained Tiffany's principal client, and his primary means of access to other viewers. The opening of the furnaces changed this, leading first to the production of a range of art glass, and then to various other art forms, which Tiffany could offer to the public through both the firm's showroom and a network of retail outlets across the country.

It remains unclear whether Tiffany foresaw at the time the huge popularity that his art glass would soon enjoy in the marketplace, or whether, as has been claimed by some art historians, the decision to extend the furnaces' production from sheet-form glass (for windows and mosaics) to the hand-blown variety was purely one of expediency: to utilize the vast inventory of glass shards that had accumulated through twenty-odd years of window production. Certainly, if the latter was the case, Tiffany could not in 1893 have envisioned the scale of the giant industrial-art manufactory that sprang up at Corona within the next ten years as a by-product of his decision to enter the domestic art market. His felicitous blend of artistic versatility and boundless energy soon led him into numerous fields of applied art, and it is interesting to consider how he perceived himself in his evolving role, from an individual artist to one increasingly preoccupied with art's application to industry. Clearly, to a purist, the two were contradictory and therefore mutually exclusive. For Tiffany the issue was one with which he had to grapple for most of his career.

In later life Tiffany justified his role as an industrial artist in prosaic terms: as fulfilling the need to introduce objects of beauty into every American home. Charles de Kay explained Tiffany's goal in *The Art Work of Louis Comfort Tiffany* (1914):

Fish Cameo vase

c. 1895. Favrile glass, 7⅛″ high
Unsigned
The National Museum of American History,
Smithsonian Institution, Washington, D.C.
Gift of Charles L. Tiffany

This vase was included in the group of early Favrile glassware donated by Tiffany's father in the mid-1890s to the Smithsonian Institution. Its wheel-engraved detailing represents the highest level of artisanship ever achieved at the Corona glassworks. It was therefore almost certainly executed by Paul Kreischman, an Austrian whom Tiffany met and hired around the time of the 1893 Columbian Exposition. Kreischman engraved other vases for Tiffany's top clients, including Gould, Havemeyer, Sage, and Vanderbilt. His premature death at age forty-five in 1898 deprived the firm of its foremost European glass artisan.

His taste in color has found expression in a thousand articles of applied art; these, occupying prominent places in households, have exercised a happy influence on the taste of citizens. It is obvious that such influences exist and make themselves felt; but that is seldom thought of. Yet the fact that things of daily use like lamps, flower-vases, and toilet articles reach a wider public than do paintings and sculpture make the "decorative" arts more important to a nation than the "fine" arts. Hence the value to a community of artists who devote their talent to making things of use beautiful. They are educators of the people in the truest sense, not as school masters laying down the law, but as masters of art appealing to the emotions and the senses and rousing enthusiasm for beauty in one's environment.

Analysis of de Kay's biography reveals several inconsistencies with this statement. Most obviously, the book was written at the moment when Tiffany's leaded-glass lamps had reached their highest domestic popularity, and, as such, constituted a substantial part of his business. Scores of lamp models were in continuous production, several in editions of over one hundred. Surely they, more than anything else manufactured by the firm, represented Tiffany's success in bringing beauty to the American home. Yet the author omitted any reference to them, while taking pains to list Tiffany's designs for textiles, furniture, photography, and landscape architecture, fields in which his achievements were often amateurish, or at best peripheral. The reason for this obvious omission tells a lot about Tiffany's determination to be perceived by posterity as an artist rather than an entrepreneur. Leaded-glass lampshades were manufactured in multiples, that is, they were mass-produced, unlike his paintings, windows, enamels, and pieces of jewelry, each of which was a *unique* work of art. The latter were therefore appropriate for a book on his artistic achievements, while the lamps clearly were not. It appears that Tiffany's reticence, or ambivalence, about the commercial nature of his business, despite its success, came to the attention of his biographer, either directly or by way of his children (who had commissioned the book for themselves), and the decision was made to omit any reference to the lamps. This may even have been a prerequisite for the book's publication.

If Tiffany had difficulty in reconciling the commercialism of his business with his preferred image, others did not. Siegfried Bing, in Paris in the mid-1890s, was one of the first to comprehend the unique potential of Tiffany's burgeoning business, and to congratulate him on his frank embrace of the machinery of mass production. He wrote in 1896 that it was "a great art industry, a vast establishment combining under the same roof an army of all kinds united by a common current of ideas. It is perhaps by the audacity of such organizations that America will prepare a glorious future for its industrial art." Certainly, it was difficult at the time to find comparable businesses anywhere. In America, nobody had attempted to produce works of art on such a scale and of such diversity. In Europe, members of the artist-artisan community in Nancy—notably, Emile Gallé, Louis Majorelle, and the Daum glassworks—were among the few others at the time occupied with the production of artworks for so broad an audience.

To some of those who visited the Corona works, Tiffany's experiment found a precedent in the doctrines of William Morris. As the critic for *Brush and Pencil* noted in 1902, "Tiffany's work has been termed the application of the maximum of ideal beauty to things utilitarian.... He is imbued, as with Morris, with a desire not merely to add to the world's beauty, but to bring that beauty within the reach of the public." Morris would have disagreed radically with Tiffany, however, on the use of mass production, rather than handcrafting, as the means to achieve their shared goal.

Only one critic, for *International Studio*, appears to have analyzed Tiffany's ambitions as naked entrepreneurship. He wrote, "We have hinted at the 'commercialism' of this big American concern; it is time to define it more closely.... 'The Tiffanys' certainly do not aim to emulate Morris & Co. in educating the public taste; their aim is to sell, to persuade, not to elevate or instruct." Clearly, this was the accusation to which Tiffany felt most vulnerable, one that he interpreted as a direct challenge to his artistic ability and integrity, even though the critic did appear to reverse himself in closing: "But no commercial considerations are allowed to stand in the way of the alert curiosity of the highly gifted artist who is the soul of the concern." Tiffany was something of a paradox: he produced handiwork on an industrial scale.

Today, while we can sympathize with Tiffany's sensitivities, we must marvel, rather, both at the sheer volume of works that were produced under his supervision—which refute absolutely his claim to be an individual artist—and at the astonishing quality of artisanship that was maintained throughout the nearly forty years that the Corona workshops were in operation. Although many objects have been lost or wantonly destroyed through the years, particularly from the 1930s until the late 1950s, when Tiffany's works were widely unfashionable, there remains such an immense inventory of his creations—from monumental windows and lamps to the smallest of accessories—that it appears that he must easily have achieved his goal to reach every American household. Not the least impressive aspect of Tiffany's legacy is the fact that his objects are readily identifiable as the work of a single hand or guiding spirit. The Tiffany influence is ubiquitous, uniting works stylistically across many mediums, including glass, bronze, enamel, ceramics, and other materials.

An aggressive marketing campaign, with sales catalogues and press releases, accompanied much of what Tiffany Studios produced, reducing further Tiffany's claim to commercial disinterest, or, at best, naivety. His former treasurer, William J. Fielding, did, however, exonerate him of crass commercialism some years ago in reporting that Tiffany Studios was invariably in the red, and that Tiffany had to write a personal check at the end of each financial year to offset the outstanding debt. Fielding portrayed a man blinded to the economic realities of the business world, one whose father's largesse subsidized his artistic ambitions. The same sentiments had been expressed in 1897 by a critic for *International Studio:* "I would suspect [him] of sometimes regarding the workshops as nothing but a splendid opportunity for trying experiments on a large scale." Today we need not concern ourselves unduly with the entrepreneurial aspects of Tiffany's firm, or with its unprofitability, and can be grateful that his father's assistance prevented the diminution of his unwavering artistic standards across so many mediums.

Favrile Glass

The Corona glassworks operated in the medium's time-honored manner, with artisans grouped in teams or "shops," headed by a master craftsman called a gaffer. Assisting him were a server, decorator, gatherer, and one or two assistants, who together orchestrated each new creation from its inception as a molten, vitreous glob to its completion. The teams worked from sketches supplied by Tiffany or the firm's designers, often creating models in small editions before changing the batches of colored glass and proceeding to another design. Production was supervised by Arthur J. Nash, who had worked for Thomas Webb & Sons in the glass-making center of Stourbridge, England, before he was invited by Tiffany around 1892 to manage the glass workshop at the new Corona plant. Assisting Nash were one or more chemists, among them Parker McIlhenny, who worked with Tiffany for twenty years. Robert Koch, in his book *Louis C. Tiffany—Rebel in Glass* (1964), recorded that there were only eight gaffers, and fewer chemists, in the entire thirty-five-year history of the Tiffany furnaces, which helps to explain the consistency of the firm's production, and the fact that designs remained largely unchanged from year to year.

A 1905 booklet titled *Tiffany Favrile Glass* listed 1893 as the year in which Tiffany introduced his hand-blown glassware, although experimentation probably proceeded for some time until he was satisfied with the overall artistic and technical quality of production. By mid-1894 he began to donate selections of art glass to museums in the United States and overseas. For two years he presented examples to over forty of the

Four red Favrile glass vases

From left, vase with molded relief decoration, 5¼" high, inscribed *L.C.TIFFANY FAVRILE 1622A*, and with original paper label; vase with iridescent surface decoration, 6" high, inscribed *9969 L.C.TIFFANY-FAVRILE*; Tel el Amarna vase with decorated collar, 9¼" high, inscribed *5966E L.C.TIFFANY-FAVRILE*; Paperweight vase decorated with trailing foliage in green and yellow, 7½" high, inscribed *445 L.C.T. FAVRILE* Collection of Howard and Paula Ellman, New York

Red Tiffany vases are prized by collectors because of their relative rarity. Such glass demanded great skill on the part of the Studios' blowers to develop the precise shade of red required for each piece. Another difficulty was that the deepest reds incorporated selenium oxide, which had a high failure rate at high firing temperatures. For its paler range of red, pink, and cranberry tones, the Studios used gold or copper chlorides or oxides, plus other ingredients, mixed in secret formulae developed through time.

Four red Favrile glass vases

world's most esteemed institutions, including the Metropolitan Museum of Art, the Smithsonian Institution, the Victoria and Albert Museum, the Imperial Museum in Tokyo, and the Louvre. Clearly a smart business ploy, these donations provided the international art community with evidence of the firm's newest venture in glass. In late 1895 Tiffany was finally ready to offer his new product to its ultimate constituency: the American consumer. A public exhibition was staged at the firm's showroom on Fourth Avenue in New York, to which the press was also invited. The critic for *The New York Herald* found the evanescent surface hues on the glassware "almost bewildering," while *The New York Times* raved about "astonishing results...entirely novel both in color and texture... absolutely unique of their kind." Tiffany named his glassware "Favrile," a derivation of the Saxon word *fabrile*, meaning "handwrought," to signify that all glass created at the Corona furnaces was hand-blown, as distinct from glass that was molded commercially.

The overwhelmingly positive response to his Favrile wares must have gratified Tiffany greatly. Gertrude Speenburg quoted him in *The Arts of the Tiffanys* (1956) on what had clearly been a long and arduous odyssey to invent glass of such range and quality:

My chemist and furnace man insisted for a long time that it was impossible to achieve the results we were striving for, claiming that the metallic oxides would not combine. That was the trouble for many years. The mix would disintegrate. New style firing ovens had to be built and new methods devised for annealing glass. By the aid of studies in chemistry and through years of experiments, I have found means to avoid the use of paints, etching, or burning, or otherwise treating the surface of the glass....I can make any shade of glass in pot metal, but it took me thirty years to learn the art.

Examination of a selection of Favrile glass shows that Tiffany's boast was not idle: by mixing up to seven colors, thrown together from different ladles, his staff could produce an inexhaustible range of blended hues, many mottled or deeply veined to simulate nature's ever-changing moods and palette. The glass was often treated with an iridescent surface finish that proved hugely popular with the public. The effect was achieved in a heating chamber, where an atomized solution of metallic vapors was sprayed onto the surface of the finished piece. The process gave a kaleidoscopic luster to the glass, one that became a principal characteristic of Favrile domestic wares.

The earliest pieces of Favrile glassware reveal Tiffany's initial reliance on traditional forms for his new medium. The majority drew inspiration from the Greek stamnos, or wine jar, krater, and tazza; the old

English possit cup; the Roman amphora; and Chinese Ming porcelain vessels, to cite some of the shapes produced between 1894 and 1896. A few showed a tentative embrace of nature in their rather stiff but organic contours, no doubt an acknowledgment by Tiffany of the Art Nouveau movement that had begun to enjoy wild popularity at the Paris salons. Tiffany never wholly rejected traditional forms, but utilized them for many of his household services, such as the Earl, Ascot, and Flemish stemware patterns. Increasingly, however, he developed a delightful range of domestic wares inspired by a floral grammar of ornament. Popular motifs included bands of striated leaves or peacock feathers applied to an iridescent-gold or cobalt-blue ground. The firm's series of flower-form vases, vessels designed as a specific flower with a broad, fluted mouth, slender tapering stem, and bulbous foot, brought Tiffany's interpretation of the European Art Nouveau style to full embodiment.

The 1900 Exposition Universelle in Paris was a triumph for Tiffany's domestic glassware production, as critics extolled the astonishing array of shapes, colors, and textures he presented. Whereas a few found it over-ripe and cloyingly sweet, almost all felt that in his Favrile wares the American had exceeded his abilities as a window maker. New techniques were being introduced continually at the time by the firm. Among the most successful were the Lava and Cypriote series; the former simulated the flow of molten gold lava over dark blue basaltic rock, the latter the surface of vessels excavated from ancient archaeological sites, in which the acids and alkalis in the soil had gradually decomposed and pitted the glass. His Agate pieces, in which layers of superimposed earth-toned colors were cut into faceted patterns that imitated those found on hardstones, were another innovation inspired by nature. From France's mid-nineteenth-century paperweight manufactories—Saint-Louis, Clichy, and Baccarat—Tiffany borrowed the Paperweight technique, in which the vase's decoration was encased, in its final visit to the fire, in a clear outer layer of glass. Related to this was another popular series of art glass, termed Aquamarine, which depicted underwater life, and which Tiffany introduced around 1911–12. Various techniques were tried continually, in the ongoing search for new artistic effects, including the use of wheel carving to achieve detailing, and the encrustation of millefiore canes into the surface of the glass. And throughout all this experimentation, an endless flow of crates, filled with functional household glassware—comports, berry dishes, epergnes, stemware, fingerbowls—was en route from Corona to retail stores across the country. Like most of the firm's operations, the production of domestic art glass became a mammoth and costly industrial undertaking that forced Tiffany to offer much of it at prices above that which the average homeowner—his professed client—could afford.

Silver-mounted vase

c. 1900. Favrile glass and silver-gilt, 5½″ high
Signed under the silver mount
Collection of Ophir Gallery,
Englewood, New Jersey

The hallmarks on the silver handles, foot, and collar of this piece are French, indicating that the mount was added to the vase after it had been shipped to France. Tiffany's closest business associate there was S. Bing, with whom he collaborated increasingly after 1893. It is therefore probable that Bing commissioned a local artist to add a mount to the vase that would increase its appeal for the local market. The choice of the cyclamen motif suggests that the design was created by Brindeau de Jarny, a Parisian sculptor noted at the time for a series of light fixtures that he had designed on the same theme. The bowl itself is a magnificent example of varicolored, iridescent Favrile glass in a watery, shimmering pattern.

Four Favrile glass vases

From left, Cypriote vase with iridescent pitted surface, 3⅞″ high, inscribed *L.C.T. 1339P*; Reactive vase with trailing prunts, 5″ high, inscribed *284G L.C.TIFFANY-FAVRILE*; Agate vase, uncut, with trapped air bubbles, 7¾″ high, inscribed *V162 L.C.TIFFANY-FAVRILE*; Lava vase, 4½″ high, inscribed *2118G L.C.TIFFANY-FAVRILE*
Collection of Howard and Paula Ellman, New York

In his Cypriote, Agate, and Lava glassware, Tiffany sought to simulate certain effects of nature: the devitrification of the surface of exhumed ancient glass in Cypriote; the duplication in glass of such hardstones as marble and chalcedony in Agate; and the flow of molten lava over basaltic rock in Lava. The example of Agate ware shown here, third from left, is a rare instance in which the glass was not cut into facets to reveal underlying layers of color. The Reactive technique, shown in a vase here, second from left, involved the application of one or more hot gathers of glass over another, which produced a chemical reaction that, in turn, created a dramatic range of color effects.

Lava vase

c. 1900. Favrile glass, 12½″ high
Inscribed *L.C.TIFFANY-FAVRILE 26A. COLL.*
Private collection

The artistic and technical importance of this vase is confirmed by its "A. Coll." designation, a category reserved by Tiffany for a select number of works (mostly in glass) created at the Corona furnaces. In all, several hundred "A. Collection" pieces are known to have been set aside for Tiffany's personal collection. These were distinguished by various criteria: unusual colorations, textures, or forms that had proven particularly difficult to achieve, or that had occurred accidentally in the manufacturing process. All "A. Coll." pieces bear one or more exceptional qualities, qualities that Tiffany decided to retain for himself, perhaps for further examination. This Lava vase came from his own collection at Laurelton Hall.

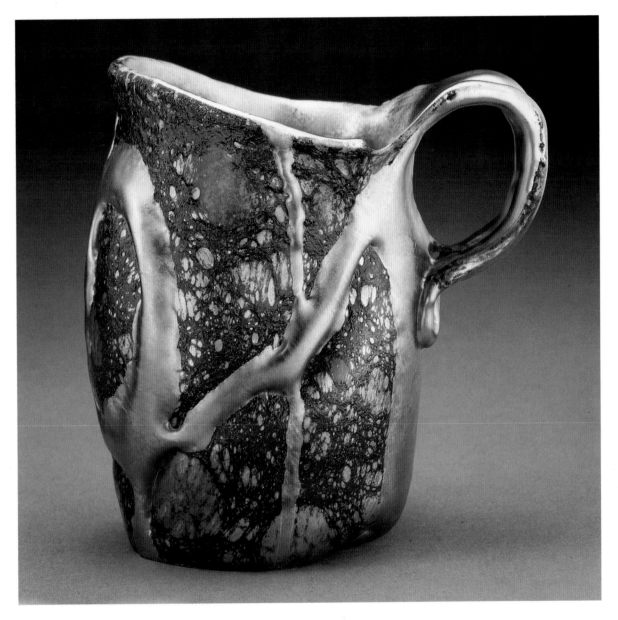

Lava ewer

c. 1910. Favrile glass, 4⅜″ high
Inscribed *L.C.TIFFANY-FAVRILE 606K*
Private collection

The rainbow iridescence on the surface of this pitcher was applied to much of the firm's household glassware. To obtain it, the piece was either sprayed with, or rotated into, a vapor of tin chloride. After this application, it was gently reheated in the furnace and left to anneal, during which process a lightly lustered metallic film formed on its surface.

Paperweight vase

c. 1905–10. Favrile glass, 8″ high
Inscribed *L.C.T. 7106A*, and with the
firm's original paper label
Private collection

*In Tiffany's Paperweight technique, the
decoration on the piece of glass was encased in an outer layer of clear glass. The
process takes its name from that employed
by France's nineteenth-century glasshouses—Baccarat, Saint-Louis, Clichy,
and Pantin—in their manufacture of
glass paperweights. Not only does the process seal the inner decoration from possible damage, but the outer layer of glass
magnifies it (the thicker the layer, the
greater the magnification), and this could
be used to achieve novel aesthetic effects.*

Eight flower-form vases

Favrile glass, tallest vase 23″ high
Private collections

*This selection shows some of the colors and
forms created by the Studios in its interpretation of nature. These vases were not
really intended to be used as receptacles
for flowers; their function was decorative.
The two in the illustration that have bulbous feet show Tiffany's successful repli-
cation of an entire plant form within a
single, fluid shape: root, stem, and petals.*

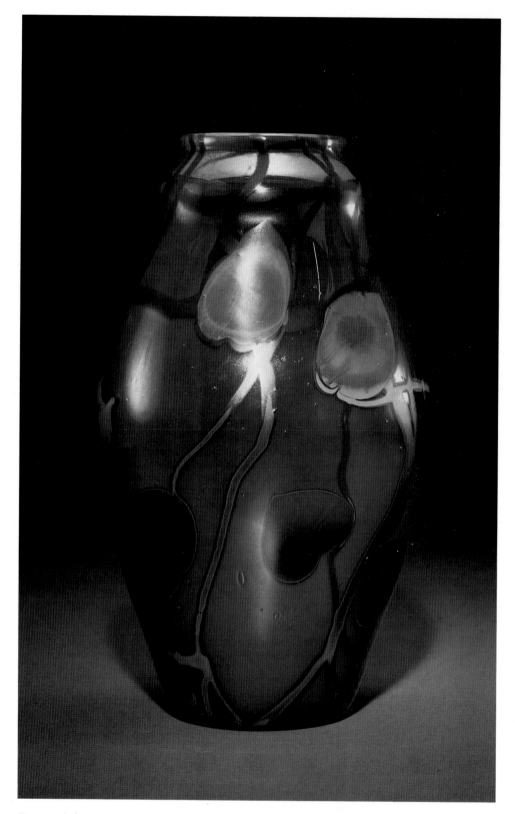

Paperweight vase

Eight flower-form vases

Silver-mounted Cameo claret jug

1906. Favrile glass and silver, 13⅜″ high
Inscribed in glass, *L.C.T. 9875A*; impressed in silver,
TIFFANY & CO MAKERS STERLING SILVER C. engraved with
the monogram *MLC* and the numbering *8834*
The Indianapolis Museum of Art. Gift of Mrs.
Carolyn A. Williams in memory of her husband,
Mr. Harry Knadler Williams, 78.269

*Tiffany utilized his father's firm for the
silver and gold mounts that he used on his
glassware in the United States. The quality of the engraving on this jug rivals that
achieved by many of the industrial art-
glass manufacturers in France at the
time, despite the fact that Tiffany employed the technique infrequently, preferring to achieve his decorative effects
within the glass while it was still molten.*

Four Favrile glass Aquamarine and Cameo vases

All c. 1912–16. From left, Aquamarine vase, 8⅞″
high, inscribed *LOUIS C. TIFFANY FAVRILE;*
Aquamarine vase, 12¼″ high,
inscribed *5209G L.C.TIFFANY-FAVRILE;*
Cameo vase, 6″ high, inscribed *X2676*; Optic vase
with engraved detailing on a shaded opalescent
ground, 8¼″ high, inscribed *L.C.T. C234*
Collection of Howard and Paula Ellman, New York

According to an article published in
American Homes and Gardens *in
1913, Tiffany had introduced his Aquamarine series of glassware roughly a year
earlier. Based primarily on images of marine life—aquatic plants, molluscs, and
fish—the pieces were encased in a thick
outer layer of glass (often tinted lightly in
a lime hue to appear more watery) that
provided the viewer with the feeling of
looking into a fishbowl or deep pond.*

Silver-mounted Cameo claret jug

Four Favrile glass Aquamarine and Cameo vases

A view of Tiffany's exhibit at the Salon of the Société des Artistes Français, Paris, 1905, showing, foreground, left and right, two enamel-on-copper pieces; and center, a pebbled Lava vase, which was later acquired by the Musée des Arts Décoratifs, the Louvre, Paris.

Lamps

There is no surviving literature in which Tiffany refers to his lamps, although he eagerly expounded his philosophy of color, light, nature, and glass in numerous speeches and articles. In the exhibition that he staged at the firm's showroom in 1916 to celebrate his sixty-eighth birthday, there was only one lamp—the unique peacock model he had designed for Charles Gould, which had a blown, rather than leaded, shade—among over 160 paintings and cabinets crammed with examples of his Favrile glassware, enameled pieces, and jewelry. Tiffany's perception of the lamps' rank commerciality caused him to feel less satisfaction with them than with most of his other artistic endeavors. Yet they were from the start immensely popular with American homeowners. Their three-dimensionality provided the perfect vehicle by which one could enjoy the spectacular, spectral qualities of Tiffany's colored glass within the confines of one's own home. Even their uncountable numbers could not obliterate the fact that they were, at their finest, a unique form of artistic expression and, as such, were easily identifiable and fashionable artifacts of interior decoration.

Tiffany's first lampshades, in the mid-1890s, were of blown glass, often supported by a matching base in which the glass was blown into a reticulated metal mount. These models preceded the commercial application of Edison's incandescent filament bulb, and were all bulky in scale due to the need for the base to enclose a fuel canister. Blown-glass shades were also created in these years for gasoliers, wall sconces, and the host of other combustion-fuel fixtures offered by the firm.

The first Tiffany lamp with a leaded, rather than blown, shade was illustrated in *Brush and Pencil* in early 1898. This had a domed shade adorned with spiraling bands of butterflies, in which each component was formed of individual pieces of flat glass held together by strips of soldered copper foil. The overall complexity of design and workmanship of the shade indicated that the process had been under development for some time. Included in the base, which was sheathed in a mosaic design of flowering primroses, was a fuel canister, which the firm was able to eliminate within a few years, as the electric incandescent filament bulb gained in dependability and durability.

A lamp brochure published by the firm in 1900 contained illustrations of a few other leaded lampshades—for example, a nautilus desk lamp and dogwood chandelier—after which production appears suddenly to have exploded, both in sheer volume and in the variety of designs offered. A 1904 booklet showed numerous important models with leaded-glass shades, including the Wisteria and large Cobweb lamp. A price

A view of the lamp department at the Corona workshops. The illustration, published in The Cosmopolitan, *January 1899, provides the earliest available documentation of the year in which the Studios began to manufacture leaded-glass lampshades. Shown are artisans assembling floral and geometric models on wooden molds.*

Tiffany's earliest lamp models, about 1896–98, included blown Favrile glass shades or simple geometric patterns executed in leaded glass. This illustration from one of the firm's lamp brochures of some years later shows a typical selection of the first lamp designs. At this time the shades were illuminated by combustion lighting, either kerosene or gas.

An early Tiffany Studios advertisement to promote its widening range of lamp models, 1903. Shown is a selection fueled by both kerosene and electricity. During this period, when many American householders were in the process of converting from combustion lighting systems in their homes to the new electricity, Tiffany Studios provided lamp buyers with its own electrification system, no doubt to allay the concerns of hesitant buyers.

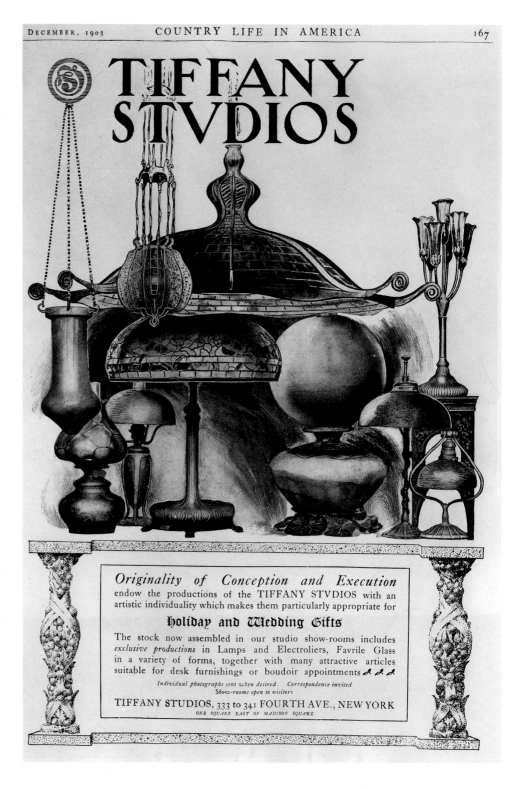

Butterfly table lamp

c. 1899. Leaded Favrile glass and enameled bronze, 26½″ high, 18⅛″ diameter of shade
Canister impressed with the Tiffany Glass & Decorating Company logo and *TIFFANY STUDIOS NEW YORK E664*
Collection of David and Catherine Bellis, Hartsdale, New York

One of the earliest recorded leaded-glass lampshades designed by the Studios (an example, with a mosaic base decorated with yellow primroses, was illustrated in Brush and Pencil *in January 1899), the butterfly model remained one of Tiffany's most popular and expensive lamps. In this example, the shade is supported by a bronze base with primroses in enameled panels within indented lines, which indicates that it may have been the prototype for those bases that were encrusted with mosaic glass tiles.*

The need for early Tiffany lamps to include within their bases a receptacle for kerosene or oil required the firm's designers to make their bases fairly bulky (such as in this model), a design constraint that disappeared when lamps were fully electrified.

list published two years later included more than three hundred models for shades and bases, many designed to be interchangeable, to accommodate the customer's individual taste. Further models, including such major examples as the Magnolia floor lamp, were introduced until 1914, after which production and client interest began to wane.

Surviving photographs of the lamp department at the Corona works reveal an assembly-line form of production, yet one in which the artisans

Butterfly table lamp

Dragonfly table lamp

c. 1900–1910. Leaded Favrile glass, mosaic, and
bronze, 17½″ high, 16″ diameter of shade
Shade model #1462; base model #147
Impressed *TIFFANY STUDIOS NEW YORK 28866*
Location unknown

Its design attributed to Clara Driscoll, from about 1899, the dragonfly lampshade became one of the Studios' most popular models and was produced subsequently in numerous sizes, colors, and shapes. The example illustrated here includes a matching base inset with mosaic glass. These mosaic bases are often considered by today's collectors to be more important, and therefore of more value, than the shades, due to their fine and detailed workmanship.

Fish-scale geometric table lamp

c. 1900–1910. Leaded Favrile glass and bronze,
29″ high, 22″ diameter of shade
Base model #392, impressed *TIFFANY STUDIOS
NEW YORK 392*
Private collection

Although most of the earliest Tiffany lamp buyers were drawn particularly to the brightly colored floral shades, as collectors are now, the Studios designed an extensive range of geometric models, which, when offered on a complementary base, presented a quiet refinement and conservatism that has an enduring appeal (to their advantage, they were also less expensive than the more intricate floral models). The fish-scale pattern on this shade is rendered in graduated shades of green to add subtlety to its impact, while the bronze base is set with a band of gold Favrile glass balls that correspond well in color with the shade.

Dragonfly table lamp

Fish-scale geometric table lamp

Clematis table lamp

Dragonfly table lamp

Dragonfly table lamp

1915. Leaded Favrile glass and bronze, 26½″ high,
20″ diameter of shade
Shade model #1495, impressed *TIFFANY STUDIOS,*
NEW YORK 1495; base model #443, impressed
TIFFANY STUDIOS, NEW YORK 443
Collection of Gallery Urban, Tokyo

Unlike most lamps, in which the shade and base have probably been interchanged at some point through the years, this shade and base are known to have been combined by Tiffany Studios, which displayed them together at the 1915 Panama-Pacific International Exposition in San Francisco. This was one of the few occasions after 1900 when the firm included examples of its lamps in an international exposition, perhaps because their wild popularity before World War I eliminated the need for them to be unduly promoted.

Clematis table lamp

c. 1900–1910. Leaded Favrile glass and bronze,
21″ high, 18″ diameter of shade
Shade model #1480, impressed *TIFFANY STUDIOS*
NEW YORK; base model #482, impressed
TIFFANY STUDIOS
Private collection

The Studios offered a wide range of interchangeable table-base models from which its clients could select one to house the shade that they had purchased. This base was also manufactured, with modifications, as a candlestick (model #1202, see the candlestick, third from left, in the illustration on page 120).

Wisteria table lamp

c. 1900–1910. Leaded Favrile glass and bronze,
27″ high, 18″ diameter of shade
Shade model #342, impressed TIFFANY STUDIOS
NEW YORK 10116; base impressed TIFFANY STUDIOS
NEW YORK 10116 4
Location unknown

The story survives that one of Tiffany's clients, a Mrs. Curtis Freschel, of Boston, approached him in 1901 with the sketch of a wisteria lamp that she wanted the Studios to manufacture for her. The completed lamp proved such a success that Tiffany requested, and obtained, Mrs. Freschel's permission to introduce it into his lamp repertoire. Very few examples have survived of a Wisteria lamp rendered in pink and burgundy tones; the vast majority are in deep blue, blue-gray, and white, sometimes heightened with yellow.

Lotus table lamp

c. 1905. Leaded Favrile glass, mosaic, and bronze,
34½″ high, 26½″ diameter of shade
Shade model #352; base impressed TIFFANY
STUDIOS NEW YORK 352
Private collection

At $750, the Lotus was the most expensive lamp model in the price list that Tiffany Studios published in 1906. Due to the time and cost involved in manufacturing it, apparently one was made at a time; only when the first was sold was a second one put into production. Three examples are known to have survived; this one is from the family of Charles Wrigley, the Chicago chewing-gum maker, who purchased it from the Tiffany Studios in the early 1900s.

Wisteria table lamp

Lotus table lamp

Nasturtium table lamp

c. 1905–10. Leaded Favrile glass and bronze, 23″ high, 18″ diameter of shade
Shade model #1533, impressed *TIFFANY STUDIOS NEW YORK 1533;* base model #179, impressed *TIFFANY STUDIOS NEW YORK 368*
Collection of David and Catherine Bellis, Hartsdale, New York

This is a particularly fine example of this model, whose flowers are rendered on a bright mottled-blue ground. The price given by the Studios of this shade in its 1906 price list was $40, which, although not excessively expensive in comparison with the firm's larger lamp models, was still beyond the reach of most households (the artisan who made it was paid roughly $15 per week, while his supervisor earned $18).

Nasturtium table lamp

Table lamp

c. 1910. Leaded Favrile glass and bronze, 30¾″ high, 21½″ diameter of shade
Shade impressed *TIFFANY STUDIOS NEW YORK;* base impressed *3476*
Collection of John and Miyoko Davey, New York

This lamp is believed to have been a unique or special-order commission, one of a number of such models that reappear intermittently on today's market without information on their provenance.

Table lamp

Sketch for a table lamp for Miss H. W. Perkins

Undated. Watercolor and pencil on paper,
15 x 11½"
Signed lower right
The Metropolitan Museum of Art, New York.
Purchase, Walter Hoving and Julia T. Weld Gifts
and Dodge Fund, 1967. 67.654.2

Tiffany's signature, bottom right, identifies the design as one of his own, a rare instance in which a lamp model (rather than a window) can be attributed with certainty to him. The Perkins lamp was executed and has survived; it is now in a New York private collection.

were provided with broad artistic latitude in their selection of glass. They were able to use their own judgment not only in the choice of textures and principal hues and intensities of the glass to be incorporated in a lamp, but in other, often indefinable considerations of color nuance and juxtaposition that would alter the aesthetic impact from one completed example to another.

Designs were divided into two broad categories: floral and geometric. The former provided a litany of garden species, of which the peony, poppy, and laburnum were perennial favorites, while the latter included a wide range of symmetrical, and therefore more conservative, designs.

HANGING · DOME · SHADE ·
· MR · J · R · MARTIN ·
· BELLEVUE · PALACE ·
· BERN · SWITZERLAND ·

Louis C. Tiffany

Sketch for a Magnolia hanging lamp for Mr. J. R. Martin of Bern, Switzerland

Probably 1910–12. Watercolor on board,
23¾ x 19¾"
Unsigned
The Metropolitan Museum of Art, New York.
Purchase, gift of Julia Weld, 1967

It is not known whether the Martin commission was executed; no example of a Magnolia dome with a lower band of pendant lily shades, such as this, has been recorded.

Others, again, such as the series of dragonfly lamp models, provided a marriage of naturalistic imagery and geometry: a band of insects on a background of repeating oblong forms. Among the most successful lamps were those in which the shade and base formed an integrated whole—for example, the Pond Lily, Lotus, Grape, Apple Blossom, and Wisteria models—in which the complete unit depicted a profusion of blossoms suspended from a central tree trunk or cluster of stems. To support its shades, the firm designed an equally diverse series of bronze bases, ranging from those inspired by botanical and zoological forms— wild carrot, cattails, peacock feathers, crabs—to those that drew directly on the grammar of traditional ornament, and used colonial, Roman, fifteenth-century, Louis XIV, and Greek decorative motifs.

Magnolia floor-lamp shade

c. 1910–15. Leaded Favrile glass, 28″ diameter
Shade model #1599, impressed *TIFFANY STUDIOS*
NEW YORK 1599
Private collection

*Accepted now as one of Tiffany's most
spectacular designs, the Magnolia floor-
lamp model was introduced at a relatively
late point in the lamp department's history, sometime between 1907 and 1913, at
a price of $300. Surprisingly, this was
well after the flower was first rendered
successfully in glass in the firm's windows
and even, possibly, after it was applied*
*as a motif on Tiffany's ceramics and
enamelwares. The use of milky glass with
variegated tints in it created the effects of
a watercolor; there is something almost
Japanese in the delicacy of this motif. As
in his bases for table lamps, Tiffany provided a range of designs for the floor-
lamp models produced by the metalware
department.*

Oriental Poppy floor-lamp shade

c. 1910–15. Leaded Favrile glass and bronze,
26″ diameter
Shade model #1902, impressed
TIFFANY STUDIOS NEW YORK 1902
Collection of Jon Peters, Beverly Hills, California

*An impressive model, due to its large size
and expanses of brightly colored blossoms,
the Oriental Poppy floor lamp was introduced by the Studios between 1906 and
1913. A similar model, decorated with
poppies rather than oriental poppies, has
blossoms concentrated in the upper half of
the shade. Both were priced at $350.*

Three enamel-on-copper items

Left, vase, 10⅞″ high, inscribed *LOUIS C. TIFFANY* and impressed *SG256*; center, covered box, 6¼″ high, inscribed *LOUIS C. TIFFANY* and impressed *SG238*; right, tray, 25½ x 14″, apparently unsigned
Private collection

The translucency of the enamel on these pieces allows the light to penetrate it and to reflect off the bright surface of the copper beneath it, which provides each piece with an enhanced luminescence.

Two enamel-on-copper vases

Left, 11¾″ high, inscribed *LOUIS C. TIFFANY SG285*; right, 6⅛″ high, inscribed *LOUIS C. TIFFANY SG45*
Private collection

Tiffany enamels usually bear one of two identification codes: EG or SG. It seems likely that SG stands for "Stourbridge Glass," the name given by Tiffany to one of the firm's two principal glass-making operations (the other was the Allied Arts Company), which were merged when the firm consolidated in 1900 under the name Tiffany Studios. There appears to be no surviving literature to identify the letters EG.

THE INDUSTRIAL ARTS

Enamelware

Tiffany appears to have set up an enameling department in 1898, as an adjunct to the firm's newly established metal foundry and workshop. Characteristically, he kept his initial experimentation under close wraps, saving its public debut for the 1900 Exposition Universelle, where it received a highly enthusiastic response. As the critic for *The China Decorator* wrote:

An entirely new and recent discovery is that of the enameling on copper, the enamel being iridescent. . . . This most difficult discovery seems to us the most wonderful of all, as there is nothing quite so difficult as enameling on metal in iridescent tones, an accomplishment not yet known here, nor indeed has precisely the same method been recorded, even in the ancient history of glass.

To achieve a sumptuous range and depth of blended naturalistic colors, Tiffany added particles of gold and silver foil to the repoussé copper body of the item under fabrication before the coats of enamel were applied. These were translucent, which allowed the light rays, on passing through them, to rebound off the mirrored foil with an enhanced brilliance. To vary the effect, other sections of the design were coated in opaque enamels, which provided contrasting areas of light and shadow. By the interplay of such light-reflective techniques and the application of an iridescent finish on the piece's last trip to the kiln, Tiffany could achieve the rich realistic effects of nature that he sought, in which his use of delicate bas-relief detailing contributed greatly.

Despite the broad popularity of Tiffany's enamels with the public and critics alike, the department remained small. Its staff in the formative years consisted of no more than a handful of young women: Julia Munson, the supervisor, Patricia Gay and Alice Goovy, enamelers, and their apprentices. Output was correspondingly small, with prices ranging from $10 for a small desk-top item to $900 for an elaborate enameled lamp base. After 1904 there were no specific references to the department in the firm's literature, although production of household accessories such as inkstands, pin trays, and vases continued, as well as of jeweled pieces, such as brooches and hair ornaments.

It appears that the department closed as quietly as it had begun, probably around 1910. It was reopened in 1920, when Tiffany Furnaces, one of two divisions set up after World War I to succeed the original Tiffany Studios, introduced a new line of enamelware (mainly desk sets) under Patricia Gay, who had been lured back from retirement.

Metalware and Fancy Goods

Tiffany appears to have relied, between 1893 and 1897, on local foundries for his metalware requirements, such as mounts for his lamps and
vases. By 1898, however, with at least three departments that required
metal components in operation—those for art glass, lamps, and enameling—it became essential for the firm to establish its own foundry at the
Corona plant. A designer, Alvin J. Tuck, was hired to supervise the new
workshop, which included sheet-metal and metal-spinning operations, in
addition to casting facilities.

Often overlooked in an examination of a Tiffany lamp or other
mounted object of art is the quality of the bronze (the firm's catalogues
listed all of its bronzeware simply as "metal"). Yet the crispness of the
casting and chasing is unerringly irreproachable, matching anything produced by the foremost American foundries of the time, the Roman
Bronze Works, Gorham, and Henry Bonnard. Finished pieces were

Two bronze inkstands

Left, 6⅛″ high, model #1066, impressed TIFFANY
STUDIOS NEW YORK; right, double inkwell, 2½″ high,
model #1070, impressed TIFFANY STUDIOS
NEW YORK D1070 3
Collection of Team Antiques,
Great Neck, New York

*Both models have a medieval, hand-
wrought look to them—the left with imita-
tion strapwork and both with exposed
rivets—reminding the viewer that Tiffany drew inspiration from classical sources
as much as from modernity. In addition,
the inkstand at left has an attached
candlestick.*

Candlestick

Bronze with amber cabochons, 7⅞″ high
Impressed *TIFFANY STUDIOS NEW YORK 702*
The Museum of Modern Art, New York.
Joseph H. Heil Fund

Unidentified in surviving Tiffany Studios literature, this model provides a fine example of Tiffany's attempt always to re-create nature precisely. Though subdued in color, it is both elegant and ornate in shape.

Selection of candlesticks

c. 1900. Bronze with Favrile glass elements
Private collections

Several of the components on these items —such as the bobeches and candle-holders—are interchangeable, allowing clients effectively to assemble a candlestick composed of their own preferred mixture of parts.

treated with one of the firm's standard patinas, usually a rich chestnut brown or greenish brown (to simulate the *verde antico* finish on works of antiquity), or electroplated in gold. It is a measure of the firm's bronzeware that collectors today concern themselves as much with the quality of a bronze Tiffany mount, and its patina, as they do with the glass that it houses.

By 1906, when the firm published a comprehensive price list of its products, the quantity of metalware objects offered was inexhaustible. Many items, such as candlesticks, were composed of interchangeable parts, such as candle shades or bobeches, which made the array even more bewildering. In addition to its bronze lamp bases and light fixtures, the firm offered a selection of table-top items—inkstands, desk sets, humidors, jewelry caskets, planters, ash receivers—grouped under the heading "Fancy Goods" and aimed at the gift market. Included in this category were deluxe creations for wealthy clients: bronze inkstands or

Selection of candlesticks

Selection of candlesticks

c. 1900. Bronze with Favrile glass elements
Left and far right, pair of candlesticks, model
#1223; second from left, Bamboo candle lamp with
glass shade, model #1206; third from left, three-
legged candlestick with glass candleholder, model
#1202 (seen also on page 105, as a lamp stand);
fourth from left, tall adjustable candlestick with
glass candleholder, 20¾″ high
Private collections

The inclusion of iridescent gold-glass ele-
ments provides these models with a richly
jeweled and therefore expensive look.

Selection of Fancy Goods

c. 1900–1910. Bronze, inset with Favrile
glass mosaic tesserae.
Back, left to right, Swirl inkwell, model #868,
Lighthouse candlestick, model #1226, and covered
box; front, left to right, Swirl pen tray, model
#1001, and Swirl paperweight, model #932
Collection of Team Antiques,
Great Neck, New York

*Desk-top objects such as these, enhanced
with colorful mosaics that were time-
consuming and costly to apply, were designed as deluxe items that the firm's
wealthiest clients could purchase as gifts.*

Scarab stamp box

c. 1900–1905. Gilt bronze with inset Favrile glass
mosaic tesserae and molded-glass scarabs,
4½ x 2¼ x 2"
Model #805, impressed *TIFFANY STUDIOS NEW YORK*
Private collection

*A fine example of the firm's line of Fancy
Goods, this box was probably inspired in
part by the Egyptian Revivalism that enjoyed a wave of popularity in Europe and
the United States toward the end of the
last century. Tiffany used the scarab
theme frequently as a decorative motif in
his jewelry and desk-top items. Here the
design on the cover includes two scarabs,
or dung beetles, with a central ball of
dung, rendered elegant and charming in
glass and gilt bronze.*

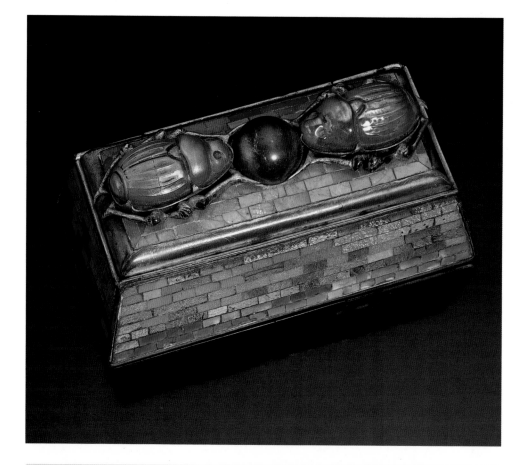

Vaporizer

c. 1900. Favrile glass with jeweled silver mount,
by Tiffany Studios and Tiffany & Company,
4½ x 1" diameter
Inscribed on rim *TIFFANY & COMPANY*
Collection of Mr. and Mrs. John W. Mecom, Jr.

*This jeweled glass perfume flask, or vin-
aigrette, made in about 1900, was one of
the initial collaborative commissions between Louis C. Tiffany and his father's
prestigious retail firm, Tiffany & Company. Upon his father's death in 1902, he
was appointed design director of the family store, and continued to design objects
that utilized the talents of both firms. This
flask, called a vaporizer, with its gem-
studded silver mount and iridescent Favrile glass body, was probably executed at
about the time of the Paris Exposition
Universelle of 1900, which was to prove
so important to Tiffany's career. A similar
jeweled vinaigrette was shown there and
included in the Pan-American Exposition in Buffalo, New York, the following
year.*

candelabra inlaid with colorful mosaic panels, glass Turtle-Back tiles, or
jeweled-glass cabochons. Also among the Fancy Goods was a delightful
selection of carved wooden humidors, playing-card boxes, and cigarette
boxes, often inset with Cypriote or gold-glass panels, which were offered
also on occasion by the family's store, Tiffany & Company, in its *Blue Book*

catalogues. The most popular of all of these household accessories were the desk sets, made in a range of Neoclassical and modern patterns, and comprising a basic number of pieces (usually seven or eight), to which the buyer could add extra units as future gifts. Some sets, such as the Grape and Pine Needle patterns, grew to over thirty in number.

Jewelry

On the death of his father in 1902, Tiffany was appointed artistic director of Tiffany & Company, a position he held until 1918. This formal link with the family's jewelry firm provided him with increased access to, and familiarity with, its jewelry-manufacturing operations, and it was predictable that his inherent curiosity and energies would lead him to explore the medium for himself.

It is difficult to determine the degree to which Tiffany utilized the facilities, materials, and staff of the Fifth Avenue store either before or after 1902. Earlier, he and his father had collaborated on several precious works, such as the vaporizer with Favrile glass body and gem-encrusted silver mounts exhibited at the 1900 Exposition Universelle, and the son's wares were offered both on the sixth floor of the store and in its annual *Blue Book* sales catalogues. Characteristically, however, Tiffany conducted his initial experiments in jewelry design in private, and the extent of the cooperation between him and his father's firm has remained uncertain. Some information has survived in the Tiffany & Company archives, yet even that—particularly on the issue of what he personally designed—is open to different interpretations.

Tiffany retained Julia Sherman to oversee his jewelry production, at first requiring her to use her name when ordering supplies in order to conceal his involvement. A small studio was established on Twenty-third Street in New York, where Sherman and her staff translated Tiffany's jewelry cartoons into finished works. It was here that Sherman crafted the jeweled and enameled gold peacock necklace that he designed for exhibition purposes. This and other early pieces were handwrought in a distinctly robust, if not rudimentary, style, far removed in spirit from the traditional jewelry manufactured at Tiffany & Company. An even greater distinction between the two was Tiffany's choice of inexpensive stones and enamels in preference to the large precious stones and lavish settings

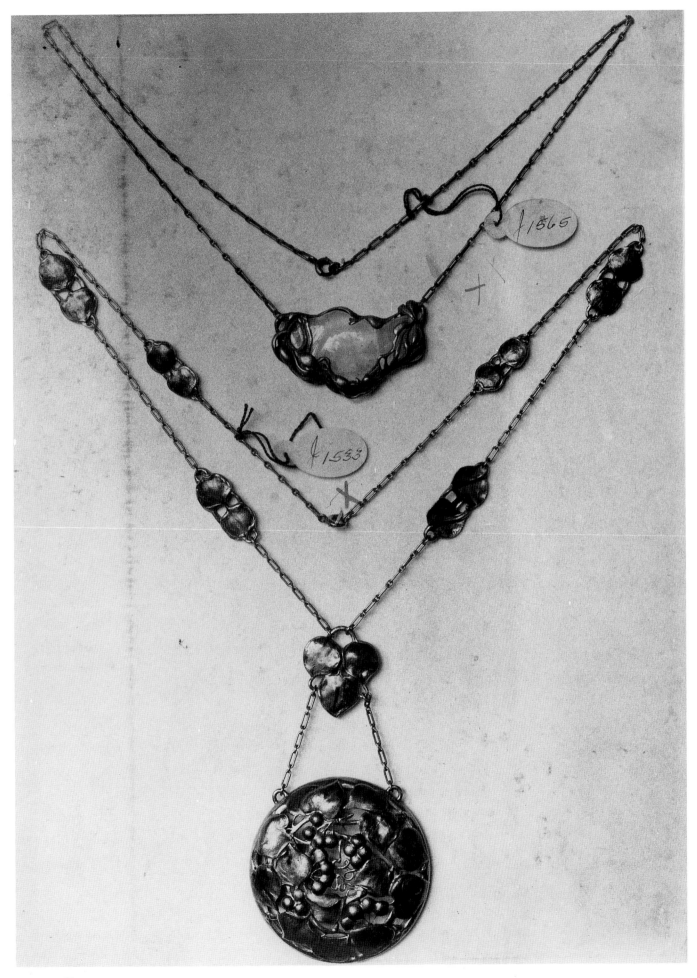

Two necklaces

Necklace

c. 1905. Seed and Baroque pearls on gold wire,
14½" long
Inscribed *LOUIS C. TIFFANY ARTIST*

A delicate composition of pearls on a gold-wire mount, this piece is similar to one that Tiffany exhibited at the Paris Salon of the Société des Artistes Français in 1905. The formality and medievalism of its design are not, however, characteristic of most of Tiffany's jewelry, which was usually more naturalistic in form and theme.

THE INDUSTRIAL ARTS

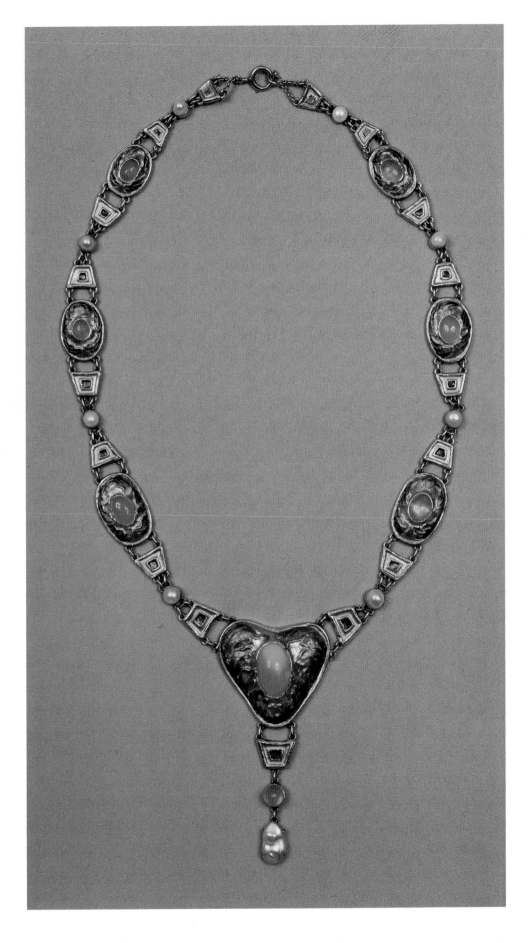

Necklace

c. 1905. Gold, enamel, opals, pearls, and
Baroque pearl, 9″ long
Inscribed LOUIS COMFORT TIFFANY
The Virginia Museum of Fine Arts, Richmond.
Gift of Sydney and Frances Lewis

Composed of Mexican opals, enameled gold, and pearls, this piece is illustrated in a photograph in the Tiffany & Company archives, proof that it was executed for Tiffany by the jewelry department in his father's firm. Whereas the handwrought and organic quality of the piece is characteristic of most of L. C. Tiffany's jewelry designs, it is less formal than, and far removed in spirit from, the jewelry that Tiffany & Company marketed under its own name and for which it became renowned in wealthy and patrician East Coast families.

Four ceramic wares

From left, Bronze Pottery vase with relief decoration, 8″ high, incised *39 A. COLL. L.C.TIFFANY FAVRILE BRONZE POTTERY*, with conjoined *LCT* monogram; vase with deep-blue and green glaze in design of pierced trailing leaves, 4″ high, incised with conjoined *LCT* monogram; light-green covered jar with floral relief decoration, 9⅜″ high, incised with conjoined *LCT* monogram; green footed bowl with relief pattern of lily pads and frogs, 6⅞″ high, incised with conjoined *LCT* monogram
Collection of Howard and Paula Ellman, New York

Many of Tiffany's ceramic wares have a sculpted three-dimensionality that he did not achieve in his glass. Both their forms and surface decoration are organic, whereas many of his glass vases and bowls were organic only in their choice of motifs; their forms were conventional to the medium. Although ceramic pieces such as these were made in limited editions, variation was achieved among examples in the same edition by the free, and therefore irregular, flow of the glaze during its application. This created subtle differences in the shading that provided a measure of individuality to each. These small vessels are not intricate or imposing, like Tiffany's windows and glasswork; they display another aspect of his style.

Ceramic vase

c. 1904–8. 8¼″ high
Inscribed *P807*
Private collection

At the suggestion of Lockwood De Forest, Tiffany taught a pottery class in 1879 at the New York Society of Decorative Arts. This indicates that he had familiarized himself with the medium well before he introduced Tiffany Studios ceramics at the Saint Louis World's Fair in 1904. Like that for his enamels and jewelry, much of his experimentation in ceramics was done in secrecy, which has kept its development at the Studios largely undocumented. This piece has a relatively simple monochrome glaze of a soft green, but its organic shape, incised surface, and celery motif are pure Tiffany style.

that were the hallmark of Tiffany & Company's creations, to provide the color and character that he sought. Following the example of the foremost European Art Nouveau jewelers, such as René Lalique and Henri Vever, Tiffany rejected the medium's conventional stones—diamonds, rubies, sapphires, and so forth—preferring modestly priced opals, tourmalines, pearls, demantoids, and carnelians. The value of his jewelry lay in its artistry and color harmonies, not in the intrinsic worth of its gemstones.

Also in common with European Art Nouveau jewelers, Tiffany chose organic themes, such as dandelions, wild carrot, grape clusters, bittersweet, blackberries, and Queen Anne's lace, for his jewelry designs. From about 1908 on, however, he appears to have contributed designs also for Tiffany & Company's own line of jewelry, and in these his distinctly naturalistic personal style is difficult to detect. Surviving examples, signed only *Tiffany & Co.* and identified in the firm's archives as by his hand, are more formal and symmetrical than the works that he displayed and marketed under his own name. The latter were shown from the early 1900s on at the annual Paris Salons, where one critic described a piece as "worthy of an amateur Lalique," a compliment that the proud Tiffany would have deemed backhanded, at best.

Pottery

It is impossible to establish precisely when Tiffany turned his attention to pottery. As in his experimentation in enameling and jewelry, he worked in secret until he felt he had achieved high artistic and technical proficiency. A reference in the journal *Keramis Studio* in 1900 hinted at preliminary tests that he had undertaken, following his examination of the display of contemporary French ceramists at the Exposition Universelle in Paris. Two years later the same magazine confirmed to its readers that Tiffany had been experimenting for some time with pottery, but it was a further two years before he invited the public, at the Saint Louis World's Fair, to view a selection of finished pieces.

Tiffany's initial interest in pottery lay partly in his need to provide bases for his glass lampshades, a need that the firms of Grueby Pottery and Rookwood met for other lamp manufacturers. Although he later abandoned the idea of ceramic lampstands, Tiffany continued to produce a range of pottery wares until about 1910, by which point production had grown uninspired, even perfunctory. By the early 1900s other American potteries were well established and included in their repertoire a range of glazes and forms similar to those with which he had experimented, and which he presumably felt were best suited artistically to the

Fern ceramic vase

c. 1905–10. 11¾″ high
Inscribed *L.C.T.*
Collection of Martin Eidelberg, New York City

Models such as this show the faithful manner in which Tiffany interpreted nature, an approach at odds with the attenuations of the European Art Nouveau movement. This example demonstrates his preference for common plants, grasses, and cereals, with which he embellished his ceramic vessels.

medium; competition from other producers no doubt led to his decision to discontinue his line. With so many monumental achievements to his name in glass, windows, lamps, enameling, and so on, Tiffany probably viewed his pottery as secondary, an opinion shared by the critics, who persistently ignored it in their reviews.

Tiffany pottery was either thrown in the traditional manner on the wheel or sculpted by hand from lumps or coils of white clay. Finishing operations included the manual application of extra ornamentation and carving and trimming to sharpen images. The piece was then molded in plaster, from which a limited edition was slip-cast. Variation was achieved by the application of different monochromatic glazes, such as mat greens, ocher, beige, ivory, and blues, or by leaving the piece in an unglazed bisque state, to allow the customer to select a finish and color, which could be done with the aid of sample tiles. For a while Tiffany also experimented with the application of a sleeve of bronze foil to the exterior of the pottery, a technique that entailed electroplating.

Tiffany's finest pottery designs were drawn directly from nature and were particularly successful when rendered in high relief with reticulated detailing. Several models were re-created from earlier repoussé enamel-on-copper wares, though their muted earth tones set them sharply apart aesthetically from their vibrant prototypes. Favorite motifs included fern fronds, cereals, toadstools, cattails, pussy willows, fish, and salamanders, although the firm also manufactured (particularly at first) a substantial number of vessels of conventional form, lightly adorned with incised or molded imagery.

The characteristics of pottery are so fundamentally different from those of glass, and draw on such opposing artistic sensitivities for their appreciation, that it is not surprising that many of Tiffany's clients were disinterested, if not disappointed, in this venture of his. Certainly, those who raved about the dramatic impact of his windows and lamps would have found his pottery flat and lifeless. The two mediums tended, for this reason, to attract different audiences, as they do today. Tiffany's pottery is appreciated for the most part by those who collect the works of other American Arts and Crafts ceramists.

Laurelton Hall

IV. The Later Years and the Pursuit of a Legacy

CHARLES LEWIS TIFFANY'S DEATH on February 18, 1902, provided Tiffany with an inheritance of roughly $3 million, a fabulous sum in the era before estate and personal income taxes. In the same year, he purchased a 580-acre parcel of land near Cold Spring Harbor and Oyster Bay, New York, overlooking Long Island Sound, a short distance from The Briars. The property included an old resort hotel, called Laurelton Hall, which was demolished to make way for a summer residence that Tiffany himself designed, and that was completed by August 1904.

Tiffany supervised every aspect of the new Laurelton Hall's construction and furnishing. It was his fourth and final home, and by far the most ambitious of them all: a country estate with a mile-long gravel driveway winding through landscaped gardens and woods to an eighty-four-room mansion, complete with coach house and stables, squash court, bowling alley, conservatory, central court, and esplanade, in addition to its standard living spaces. As a measure of the professionalism with which he approached the project, Tiffany prepared a preliminary scale model of the site in clay and wax that included all of its topographical features. The position of the house was chosen to integrate it fully into its surroundings.

The building defied strict architectural classification, which should be no surprise, coming from an artist-designer who had established his reputation as a nonconformist. Although most of its identifiable elements were neo-Islamic—Tiffany described them as Persian—the building as a whole reflected Tiffany's proven eclecticism. Samuel Howe observed in *Appleton's Magazine* in 1907 that Tiffany had "refused to yield to the imprisonment of [a] historic style...so false to the ideals of our civilisation...the painter determined to work alone and fight out the problem in his own way." In sum, the structure represented a unique and distinctly personal architectural statement in which influences were scrambled or juxtaposed as Tiffany saw fit: for example, the Chinese-style dining room led into a smoking room crammed with the Japanese and Native American artifacts he had collected for years, while on the portico Moorish

The main entrance and loggia of Laurelton Hall, which faced away from the waterfront at Cold Spring Harbor. The loggia was formed of two freestanding columns and two pilasters, surmounted by cement capitals inset with bands of red ceramic poppies raised on green glass stems. These supported a decorated pediment. Although the house was badly damaged by fire in 1957, the columns, and the three hanging lanterns flanking them, designed by Tiffany, are now installed in the sculpture garden in the American Wing at the Metropolitan Museum of Art, New York.

133

The dining room at Laurelton Hall, c. 1912. More formal and restrained than most of the rooms in the mansion, it contained one large and two small tables, with chairs, that were Oriental in style, all designed by Tiffany. The room was lit primarily by a large chandelier decorated with a medallion pattern that matched the room's blue wool carpets. Three clocks on the chimneypiece displayed the hour, day, and month.

arches were surmounted by vibrant glass floral capitals, made at the Corona glassworks.

Elsewhere, a music room served as the mansion's artistic inner sanctum, its walls enclosing several of Tiffany's favorite windows: either originals that Tiffany Studios had reserved for exhibition purposes and never offered for sale, or exact copies of windows that Tiffany had executed for important clients in his early years and later replicated for his own enjoyment. Included were the four individual panels from the *Four Seasons* window that had flanked the entrance to the United States pavilion at the 1900 Exposition Universelle in Paris; a copy of the eggplant overdoor transom that he had designed for the George Kemp residence in 1879; a copy of the dining-room transom he had designed for Mary Elizabeth Garrett in 1885; and the *Bathers* window, designed for the 1915 Panama-Pacific International Exposition in San Francisco, but installed directly in Laurelton Hall after Tiffany and the exposition's management disagreed on how to display it there.

Tiffany began, in this way, to surround himself at Laurelton Hall with a permanent collection of his works, one that would serve to document some of the highlights of his long career as a multitalented artist-designer. Elsewhere in the mansion, groups of vases and hanging light fixtures likewise were vivid reminders of techniques at first impossible in their complexity and later mastered.

In his desire to gather to himself a collection of his masterpieces, Tiffany made the decision in 1916 to reacquire the chapel he had exhibited at the 1893 Columbian Exposition. The chapel had been purchased from Tiffany Studios by a Chicago philanthropist, Celia Whipple Wallace, upon its return to New York, and then donated to the Cathedral of Saint John the Divine, in New York, where it had been allowed to languish and deteriorate in a side crypt. A building was now constructed on the grounds at Laurelton Hall to house the chapel, its installation helping further to establish Tiffany's new home as the final repository of his life's work.

It appears that by 1913, when Tiffany was sixty-five years old, he had begun to plan both his retirement and the legacy by which he wished the world to remember him. Part of this had been achieved in the construction of Laurelton Hall, whose massive scale and splendor embodied his success, and in the assemblage and display there of his personal collections of art, comprising paintings, ancient Roman glass, Native American artifacts, Chinese and Japanese ceramics, metalware, rugs, and prized works by his own hand. Tiffany clearly felt, however, that whereas these together exemplified his connoisseurship and artistry, they were not in themselves enough to consolidate his reputation.

Tiffany dressed as a Mideastern potentate for the Egyptian pageant-masque that he staged at the Tiffany Studios showroom, 345 Madison Avenue, New York, on February 4, 1913. It was a lavish and spectacular affair in which guests also dressed in exotic costumes. The evening's chief entertainment was a pantomime, designed by the amateur Egyptologist Joseph Lindon Smith, that depicted a romantic interlude between Cleopatra and Marc Antony. This was followed by an eight-course meal.

To ensure still further recognition of his achievements, he initiated in 1913 the first of a series of grand fêtes, or pageants, to which New York's high society—not only its wealthiest citizens, and among them his clients, but its foremost writers, actors, artists, and politicians—were invited. The first of these staged events was an Egyptian masque, held on February 4, 1913, at the Tiffany Studios showroom on Madison Avenue. A grand affair, it was planned to the tiniest detail, with invitations written on scrolls in hieroglyphics, accompanied by an English translation. Guests

A group of guests at the 1913 Egyptian pageant-masque. Those invited were advised in advance where they could rent costumes that Tiffany is said to have vetted previously. Following a re-creation of Marc Antony's return to Cleopatra in Alexandria—replete with a host of costumed fakirs, jugglers, fortune-tellers, merchants, fruit vendors, eunuchs, and priests—the guests were served a champagne dinner catered by Delmonico's.

Tiffany in his late sixties or early seventies, around 1915–20.

THE LATER YEARS

were required to attend in period costume, which they could rent or purchase for the occasion. Surviving photographs reveal Cleopatra, surrounded by assorted attendants, arriving by palanquin to receive Marc Antony; Ruth St. Denis performing Eastern dances; and the bearded host, clad as an Oriental potentate, smiling benignly on the festivities. As splendid as it clearly was, the evening was perceived by some as an attempt by Tiffany to cling to the limelight at a time when his art had begun to appear outmoded, an observation given credence less than two weeks later with the opening of the highly controversial, and now famous, Armory Show at the Sixty-ninth Regimental Armory in Manhattan. The inaugural presentation in America of paintings and sculpture by Europe's foremost abstractionists—works in which form and the organization of shapes and colors superseded traditional representations, such as the depiction of nature—shocked not only the public at large, but Tiffany himself. Later writing in *The World* (February 27, 1916), he denounced these Modernists as those who "wander after curiosities of technique, vaguely hoping they may light on some invention which will make them famous. They do not belong to art; they are not artists; they are untrained inventors of processes of the arts." This harsh denunciation, coming as it did from an artist who had always prided himself on being a fierce individualist, if not a rebel, and one who had sought innovation and originality in place of academic conformity, smacked at the very least of insensitivity, if not outright hypocrisy. Perceiving himself now as a patriarch within the artistic community, Tiffany failed to understand, or to remember, that each new generation—as had his own in the early 1870s—challenges and reevaluates its cultural inheritance.

Tiffany organized two further events in the next few years. The first was a dinner, held on May 15, 1914, for which 150 prominent New Yorkers traveled by private train from Pennsylvania Station to Oyster Bay, and from there to Laurelton Hall. For those, especially, who had never visited Tiffany's summer home, the event was highly memorable: the beds of flowers were in full spring bloom, while wisteria and laurel hung from the pergolas lining the esplanade. It was, as Tiffany had carefully planned, a setting of perfect beauty. The dinner itself, served in part by the Tiffany children dressed in Grecian costumes, included a main course of peafowl.

In the same year a biography of Tiffany, titled *The Art Work of Louis C. Tiffany*, was published. Ostensibly written by a close friend, Charles de Kay, but in effect a ghosted autobiography, the volume was published in an edition of 502 copies, each hand bound and numbered. Individual copies were inscribed and presented by Tiffany to those—family, friends, and institutions—who would appreciate the message of his art.

Four generations of Tiffanys: seated, Louis Comfort Tiffany with his great-grandson, Henry B. Platt, on his lap; standing, from left, his eldest daughter, Mary Tiffany Lusk and her daughter, Louise Lusk Platt; taken at the Tiffany vacation home in Florida, 1925.

Tiffany on the beach in southern Florida with his granddaughter, Louise Lusk Platt, left, and Sarah Handley, 1930. Handley, an Irish nurse, was retained when Tiffany became ill in 1910, after which she stayed on, eventually becoming his constant companion. Although lacking in formal education, she helped to manage Laurelton Hall and the Louis Comfort Tiffany Foundation. She later declined Tiffany's offer of marriage (he had been widowed for the second time in 1904) out of consideration for the family's feelings. After he died, she spent her remaining years in a house that he had built for her near Laurelton Hall.

A final masque, titled "Quest of Beauty," was staged in February 1916 to celebrate Tiffany's sixty-eighth birthday. This coincided with a retrospective exhibition at Tiffany Studios of over 160 paintings, with small selections of glassware, enameled pieces, ceramics, and jewelry, reminding his guests yet again of his prodigious output and versatility.

In the following year Tiffany began to formulate plans for the most ambitious and important element of his legacy: a foundation bearing his name that would, in his words, "stimulate love of beauty and imagination by giving free play to the development of individual artistic personality."

The Louis Comfort Tiffany Foundation was incorporated in 1918. Tiffany endowed it with the Laurelton Hall mansion and 62.1 acres of accompanying land, all of his art collections, the 1893 chapel, and $1.5 million in funding. Established young artists from any field of endeavor—designers, printmakers, sculptors, photographers, painters—were invited to a residency at Laurelton Hall for a month (later extended to two) to pursue research with little formal instruction. The foundation's charter defined its specific goals: "The nature of the institution to be founded is an art institute, the object and purposes of which are art education directed toward both art appreciation and production, within the scope of the industrial as well as the fine arts and as one means toward these educational purposes the establishment and maintenance of a museum to contain objects of art."

Here, finally, was the vehicle by which Tiffany's art would achieve a high place: through an art colony of disciples who would later promulgate his philosophies to the outside world. As Neil Harris has noted, the foundation provided Tiffany with his final career, "that of teacher, pedagogue, master, and host, the presiding genius of a group of acolytes who could spread the gospel in years to come." Like Frank Lloyd Wright at Taliesin and Elbert Hubbard at Roycroft, Tiffany had, at Laurelton Hall, created the means to perpetuate his name.

The Louis Comfort Tiffany Foundation became operational at Laurelton Hall on May 1, 1920. Its first artists in residence were eight male students; women were admitted from 1922. The program continued as planned throughout the 1920s, with Tiffany himself often on hand to view finished works. Some courses were conducted between May and October, following which the works of present and past participants were exhibited and offered for sale during the winter at the Art Center gallery at 65 East Fifty-sixth Street, New York.

The foundation's endowment, and with it its goals, was sharply diminished following the stock-market crash of 1929, in which the value of its portfolio fell by 33 percent. Tiffany's personal fortune had in the previous years likewise been depleted, in large part by the debts owed to him

Tiffany at Laurelton Hall, holding his first great-grandson, Henry B. Platt, born to Collier and Louise Lusk Platt, in June 1924. Platt is the last Tiffany descendant to have worked at Tiffany & Company. He joined the firm in 1947 and retired in 1981, having served both as president and as chairman.

by the Tiffany Studios, funds that he never recovered (the Studios were declared bankrupt in 1932). After his death on January 17, 1933, the foundation remained in full operation, even after Laurelton Hall itself was closed in 1938, until the United States entered World War II. At that point it too began to unravel; in late 1946 the art collections from Laurelton Hall were sold at public auction by the Parke-Bernet Galleries in New York. Three years later, the building itself and four accompanying acres of land were sold for $10,000, the paltry price explained by the fact that the building was simply too large for prospective buyers, and far too expensive to maintain.

The final curtain on Tiffany's dream home was yet to come, however; a series of fires, set probably by vandals, broke out in the mansion in 1957 and raged for three days. Fortunately, parts of the building escaped the fire. From these, a former student of the Louis Comfort Tiffany Foundation, Hugh McKean, and his wife, Jeannette, were invited by the Tiffany family to salvage as many Tiffany artworks—including the chapel and numerous windows—as they wished. These were driven by truck to Winter Park, Florida, where they are now on exhibit at McKean's institution, the Morse Museum of American Art. Through all of these reversals, the foundation has survived, albeit in somewhat diminished form, and today provides roughly $100,000 in annual grants to gifted artists, a sponsorship of which its founder would no doubt approve, despite its reduced scale.

After his death, interest in Tiffany's artworks lay dormant for three decades. Only in the mid-1960s was there a discernible revival in their popularity, pioneered by New York art dealers such as Martin Grossman and Lillian Nassau, and by the publication of a fine biography of Tiffany by Robert Koch. Tiffany had suffered the cyclical fate of many great artists: a first generation loved and bought his work; a second reviled and rejected it fully; and a third rediscovered its magical charms. Today it is difficult to comprehend how it ever fell from grace, or how it could ever do so again. Tiffany's legacy has not only survived, but thrived, not through the foundation that he painstakingly endowed to ensure that it would, but by the sheer beauty of the objects themselves.

Tiffany in Miami, 1930. Increasingly from the early 1920s, as he adjusted to semiretirement, Tiffany spent the winters in southern Florida, where he socialized with, among others, Thomas Edison, whose winter home was in Fort Myers, northwest of Miami.

Chronology

1848	Louis Comfort Tiffany born in New York on February 18, son of Charles Lewis Tiffany, owner of the Tiffany & Company store
1866–67	Enrolls at the National Academy of Design, New York
c. 1867	Makes the acquaintance of George Inness, under whom he studies informally
1868–69	Studies painting in Europe under Léon Bailly
1870	Elected a member of the Century Club, New York. Meets Samuel Colman. Visits Cairo
1871	Elected an associate member of the National Academy of Design
1872	Marries Mary Woodbridge Goddard, May 15
1873	First experiments in glass making at New York commercial glasshouses, including Heidt, Thill, Dannenhoffer, and Leo Popper. Birth of first daughter, Mary, April 3
1874	Birth of first son, December 9; dies three weeks later in Menton, France
1876	Exhibition of paintings at Philadelphia Centennial Exposition; National Academy of Design, New York; and the Century Club, New York. Executes first ornamental windows
1878	Exhibition of paintings at the Exposition Universelle, Paris. First completed window commission, for Saint Mark's Episcopal Church, Islip, New York. Establishes residence at Bella Apartments, 48 East Twenty-sixth Street, New York. Elected treasurer of the Society of American Artists. Birth of son, Charles Lewis II, January 7
1879	Forms his first business, L. C. Tiffany & Associated Artists, an interior-decorating firm, in partnership with Samuel Colman, Lockwood De Forest, and Candace Wheeler. Birth of second daughter, Hilda, August 24. Commission for George Kemp's Fifth Avenue residence
1880	Elected a full member of the National Academy of Design. Commission for the interior decoration of the Veterans Room and library in the Seventh Regiment Armory on Park Avenue, New York. Commission for the drop curtain, Madison Square Theater, New York. First experiments with mosaics; first wallpaper designs
1880–81	Commission for the entrance stairway and halls, Union League Club, New York
1881	Registers patent for opalescent window glass
1881–82	Commissions for William S. Kimball residence, Rochester, New York; Mark Twain residence, Hartford, Connecticut; Cornelius Vanderbilt II mansion, New York; Ogden Goelet residence, New York; W. H. De Forest dining room, Kingscote dining room, J. Taylor Johnston parlor, William T. Lusk dining room, all New York
1882–83	Commission to decorate the White House under President Arthur
1883	Termination of L. C. Tiffany & Associated Artists
1884	Death of Tiffany's first wife, Mary, January 22

1885	Forms new firm, the Tiffany Glass Company. Decorates the Lyceum Theater, New York
c. 1885	Construction of the Tiffany mansion at Seventy-second Street and Madison Avenue, New York, in collaboration with Stanford White
1886	Second marriage, to Louise Wakeman Knox, November 9
1888	The Kempner Memorial window installed in Saint Paul's Episcopal Church, Milwaukee, Wisconsin (Tiffany's largest figural window)
1889	Travels extensively through Europe. Chittenden window commission for Yale University, New Haven, Connecticut
1890	Experiments with glass tiles
c. 1890	Construction of The Briars country estate, Oyster Bay, New York
1890–92	Redecorates Henry O. Havemeyer house
1892	Forms the Tiffany Glass & Decorating Company and establishes a glass furnace in Corona, New York
1893	Participates in the Columbian Exposition in Chicago; display includes a chapel, other liturgical works, and domestic windows. Tiffany Glass & Decorating Company is awarded fifty-four medals
c. 1893	Tiffany's glass manufacturing operation divided into the Stourbridge Glass Company and the Allied Arts Company
1894	Applies to the United States Patent Office to register the trademark *Favrile* to be used on all items made by the company. Exhibition of glassware at the Salon of the Société Nationale des Beaux-Arts, Paris
1894–97	First sales of Favrile glassware, including vases and lamps with blown-glass shades. Fifty-three pieces of Favrile glassware donated to the Metropolitan Museum of Art by Henry O. Havemeyer. Thirty-eight pieces of Favrile glassware sold to the Smithsonian Institution, Washington, D.C. Twenty-three pieces of Favrile glassware sent to the Imperial Museum of Fine Arts, Tokyo
1895	Exhibition at the Salon of the Société Nationale des Beaux-Arts, Paris, including a selection of Favrile glassware and of windows designed by Paul Albert Besnard (*La Cascade*), Pierre Bonnard (*La Maternité*), Ker-Xavier Roussel (*Le Jardin*), Paul Ranson (*La Moisson fleurie*), P.-A. Isaac (*Iris et Roseaux*), H.-G. Ibels (*L'Eté*), Edouard Vuillard (*Les Marronniers*), Maurice Denis (*Une Paysage*), Henri de Toulouse-Lautrec (*Papa Chrysanthème*), Félix Vallotton (*Une Parisienne*), and Paul Sérusier (three untitled panels), executed by Tiffany
1895–96	Exhibition of Favrile glassware and windows designed by Eugène Grasset and Sérusier, at S. Bing's gallery, L'Art Nouveau, in Paris
1896	Commission for Pratt Institute library, New York

1896–97	Exhibition of Favrile glassware at the Salon of the Société Nationale des Beaux-Arts, Paris
1897	Publication of a list of completed Tiffany window commissions
1897–98	Exhibition at the Salon of La Libre Esthétique, Brussels
1898	Opening of a Tiffany showroom at 331–341 Fourth Avenue, New York. Commission for the Art Institute of Chicago
1898–99	Exhibition of Favrile glassware and an electric lamp at Bing's gallery, L'Art Nouveau. Forms an enameling department
1899	Exhibition at the Grafton Galleries, London, of windows, lamps, and glassware. First documentation of a leaded-glass lamp (a butterfly model)
1900	Participates in the Exposition Universelle, Paris, with more than one hundred pieces of glassware, windows, lamps, mosaics, and enamels. Awarded several Grand Prizes by the exposition jury and appointed knight of the Legion of Honor by the French state. Changes the firm's name from Tiffany Glass & Decorating Company to Tiffany Studios. Commission for the Chicago Public Library
1901	Participates in the Pan-American Exposition, Buffalo, New York, and in Saint Petersburg, Russia; awarded a Grand Prize at both. First Wisteria lamp designed by Mrs. Curtis Freschel
1902	Appointed design director of Tiffany & Company on the death of his father, Charles Lewis Tiffany. Relocation of Tiffany showroom to Forty-fifth Street, New York. Formally adopts the name Tiffany Studios for all items made at the Corona factory. Participates in the Turin World Exposition, Italy; awarded the Grand Prize for his lily-cluster lamp model. Tiffany Furnaces established
1902–4	Constructs a summer home, Laurelton Hall, near Oyster Bay on the north shore of Long Island
1904	Death of his second wife, Louise, May 9. Exhibits at the Saint Louis International Exposition
1905	Exhibits at the Salon of the Société des Artistes Français, Paris
1906	Publishes a Tiffany Studios price list, providing a comprehensive listing by model number of lampshades, bases, candlesticks, Fancy Goods, and desk sets. Exhibits at the Salon of the Société des Artistes Français, Paris
c. 1910	Publishes "A Partial List of Windows," an updated (but incomplete) list of completed Tiffany Studios window commissions (primarily ecclesiastical)
1911	Completes a glass-mosaic curtain for the National Theater in Mexico City
1912	Peacock and cockatoo glass panels for Captain J. R. DeLamar installed in his Madison Avenue residence, New York
1912–14	Constructs the mosaic murals and domes for the Roman Catholic cathedral in Saint Louis, Missouri, consisting of 30 million pieces of glass mosaic
1913	Exhibits at the Salon of the Société des Artistes Français, Paris. Publishes an updated version of the 1906 Tiffany Studios price list of lamps, bases, etc., including models introduced in the

interim. Egyptian Fête at Tiffany Studios showroom. Visits Nuremberg, Germany. Visits Havana, Cuba, to oversee large domestic window commission

1914	Biography of Tiffany by Charles de Kay, titled *The Art Work of Louis C. Tiffany*, published. Exhibits at the Salon of the Société des Artistes Français, Paris. Creates *The Bathers* window, later installed in Laurelton Hall. Queen Anne's Lace design patented, February 3. Gala Feast at Laurelton Hall
1915	Participates in the Panama-Pacific International Exposition in San Francisco. Creates *Dream Garden* mosaic mural, designed by Maxfield Parrish, for the lobby of the Curtis Publishing Company building in Philadelphia
1916	Retrospective exhibition of Tiffany paintings, glassware, mosaics, enamels, and lamps, at Tiffany Studios showroom, to celebrate Tiffany's sixty-eighth birthday; "Quest of Beauty" birthday party at the Tiffany Studios showroom. Tiffany's mosaic chapel from the 1893 Columbian Exposition, which had been installed in 1899 in a crypt of the Cathedral of Saint John the Divine, New York, reinstalled at Laurelton Hall. Visits Alaska
1918	Creates the Louis Comfort Tiffany Foundation to subsidize gifted young artists
1919	Retires and roughly divides Tiffany Studios into Tiffany Furnaces, which is taken over by A. Douglas Nash for the continued production of Favrile glassware, and the Tiffany Ecclesiastical Department, which continues the firm's production of windows, mosaics, leaded lamps, etc., under the name of Tiffany Studios
1922	Creates the *Te Deum Laudamus* mosaic triptych for the First United Methodist Church, Los Angeles
1924	L. C. Tiffany Furnaces dissolved
1927	Collection of Tiffany glass presented to Andrew Dickson White Museum of Art at Cornell University, Ithaca, New York
1932	Tiffany Studios declares bankruptcy
1933	Death of Louis Comfort Tiffany, January 17. Westminster Memorial Studios established by former employees to complete outstanding Tiffany Studios commissions
1934	First of several public auctions to dispose of the firm's inventory
1946	Contents of Laurelton Hall sold at public auction in New York
1957	Laurelton Hall partially destroyed by fire
1958	First important retrospective exhibition of Tiffany's work, at the Museum of Contemporary Crafts, New York
1967	Heckscher Museum exhibition, Huntington, New York
1979	Grey Art Gallery and Study Center, New York University, exhibition of paintings
1989–90	Exhibition, "Masterworks of Louis Comfort Tiffany," at the Smithsonian Institution, Washington, D.C., and the Metropolitan Museum of Art, New York
1991	Traveling exhibition, "Masterworks of Louis Comfort Tiffany," in Japan, with venues in Tokyo, Kobe, Nagoya, and Toyama

Bibliography

Books

AMAYA, MARIO. *Tiffany Glass.* New York: Walker and Sons, 1966.

BING, S. *La Culture artistique en Amérique.* Paris: privately printed, 1896.

BURLINGHAM, MICHAEL JOHN. *The Last Tiffany: A Biography of Dorothy Tiffany Burlingham.* New York: Atheneum, 1989.

DE FOREST, LOCKWOOD. *Domestic Indian Architecture.* Boston: Heliotype Printing Co., 1885.

DE KAY, CHARLES. *The Art Work of Louis C. Tiffany.* New York: Doubleday, Page, 1914.

DUNCAN, ALASTAIR. *Tiffany at Auction.* New York: Rizzoli, 1981.

———. *Tiffany Windows.* New York: Simon and Schuster, 1980.

DUNCAN, ALASTAIR; EIDELBERG, MARTIN; and HARRIS, NEIL. *Masterworks of Louis Comfort Tiffany.* New York: Harry N. Abrams, 1989.

FELDSTEIN, WILLIAM J., JR., and DUNCAN, ALASTAIR. *The Lamps of Tiffany Studios.* New York: Harry N. Abrams, 1982.

GARNER, PHILIPPE. *Glass 1900: Gallé, Tiffany, Lalique.* London: Thames and Hudson, 1979.

GROVER, RAY and LEE. *Art Glass Nouveau.* Rutland, Vermont: Tuttle, 1968.

ISHAM, SAMUEL. *The History of American Painting.* New York: Macmillan, 1905.

KOCH, ROBERT. *Louis C. Tiffany—Rebel in Glass.* 3d ed. New York: Crown, 1982.

———. *Louis C. Tiffany's Glass, Bronzes, Lamps.* New York: Crown, 1971.

———. *S. Bing, Artistic America, Tiffany Glass and Art Nouveau.* Cambridge, Massachusetts, 1970.

MCKEAN, HUGH. *The "Lost" Treasures of Louis Comfort Tiffany.* New York: Doubleday, 1980.

———. *Treasures of Tiffany.* Exh. cat. Chicago: Museum of Science and Industry, 1982.

METROPOLITAN MUSEUM OF ART. *Art Nouveau: Art and Design at the Turn of the Century.* New York: Doubleday, 1935.

NEUSTADT, EGON. *The Lamps of Tiffany.* New York: Fairfield Press, 1970.

PAUL, TESSA. *The Art of Louis Comfort Tiffany.* London: Quintet, 1987.

POTTER, NORMAN, and JACKSON, DOUGLAS. *Tiffany.* London: Octopus, 1988.

PURTELL, JOSEPH. *The Tiffany Touch.* Kingsport, Tennessee: Kingsport Press, 1971.

REVI, ALBERT CHRISTIAN. *American Art Nouveau Glass.* New York: Thomas Nelson and Sons, 1968.

SELZ, PETER. *Art Nouveau.* Exh. cat. New York: Museum of Modern Art, 1960.

SHELDON, GEORGE W. *Artistic Houses.* New York: D. Appleton, 1882–84.

SPEENBURGH, GERTRUDE. *The Arts of the Tiffanys.* Chicago: Lightner, 1956.

STODDARD, WILLIAM O. *The Tiffanys of America: History and Genealogy.* New York: Nelson Otis Tiffany Publisher, 1901.

VAN TASSEL, VALENTINE. *American Glass.* New York: Gramercy, n.d.

WHEELER, CANDACE. *Yesterdays in a Busy Life.* New York: Harper and Brothers, 1918.

Magazine Articles, Periodicals, and Pamphlets

CONWAY, EDWARD HAROLD. "Mr. Louis C. Tiffany's Laurelton Hall at Cold Spring, Long Island." *The Spur.* August 15, 1914, 25–29.

DAY, LEWIS F. "Favrile Glass." *Magazine of Art* 24 (1900): 541–44.

DE QUELIN, RENÉ. "A Many-Sided Creator of the Beautiful." *Arts and Decoration* 17 (1911): 176–77.

FRED, A. W. "Interieurs von L. C. Tiffany." *Dekorative Kunst* 9 (1901): 110–16.

HARRISON, CONSTANCE CARY. "Some Work of the Associated Artists." *Harper's Magazine* 69 (1884): 343–51.

HARVEY, JAMES L. "Source of Beauty in Favrile Glass." *Brush and Pencil* 9 (January 1902): 167–76.

HOWE, SAMUEL. "The Dwelling Place as an Expression of Individuality." *Appleton's Magazine* (February 1907): 156–65.

———. "The Long Island Home of Mr. Louis C. Tiffany." *Town and Country*. September 6, 1913, 24–26, 42.

LOTHROP, STANLEY. "Louis Comfort Tiffany Foundation." *American Magazine of Art* 14 (1923): 615–17.

"Louis C. Tiffany and His Work in Artistic Jewelry." *The Jewelers' Circular* 30 (December 1906): 33–42.

LOUNDSBERY, ELIZABETH. "Aquamarine Glass." *American Homes and Gardens* (December 1913): 418, 441.

MCKEAN, HUGH F. "Laurelton Hall: Tiffany's Art Nouveau Mansion." Winter Park, Florida: Rollins Press, 1977.

———. "Louis Comfort Tiffany as I Remember Him." Winter Park, Florida: Rollins Press, 1977.

———. "A Study of Louis Comfort Tiffany." *Flamingo* 31 (Winter 1955).

SAYLOR, HENRY H. "The Country Home of Mr. Louis C. Tiffany." *Country Life in America* (December 1908): 157–62.

SYFORD, ETHEL. *Examples of Recent Work from the Studio of Louis C. Tiffany*, Tiffany Studios booklet, 1911. Reprinted from *New England Magazine*, n.s. 45 (September 1911): 97–108.

Tiffany Glass & Decorating Company. *A List of Windows and Extracts from Letters and Newspapers*, 1897.

———. *A Synopsis of the Exhibit at the World's Fair, Chicago*, 1893.

———. *Tiffany Favrile Glass*, 1896.

———. *Tiffany Glass Mosaics*, 1896.

"Tiffany Glass and Decorating Company's Exhibit at the Columbian Exposition." *Decorator and Furnisher* 23 (October 1893): 9–12.

Tiffany, Louis C. "American Art Supreme in Colored Glass." *The Forum* 15 (1893): 621–28.

———. "Color and Its Kinship to Sound." *The Art World* 2 (1917): 142–43.

———. "The Gospel of Good Taste." *Country Life in America* 19 (November 1910): 105.

———. "The Quest of Beauty." *Harper's Bazaar* (December 1917): 43–44.

———. "What Is the Quest of Beauty?" *International Studio* 58 (April 1916): lxiii.

Tiffany Studios. *Bronze Lamps*, 1904.

———. *Character and Individuality in Decorations and Furnishings*, 1913.

———. *Memorials in Glass and Stone*, 1913.

———. *A Partial List of Windows*, 1910.

———. *Tiffany Favrile Glass*, 1905.

TOWNSEND, HORACE. "American and French Applied Art at the Grafton Galleries." *The Studio* 17 (1899): 39–46.

WAERN, CECILIA. "The Industrial Arts of America: I. The Tiffany Glass and Decorating Co." *The Studio* 9 (1897): 156–65.

———. "The Industrial Arts of America: II. The Tiffany or 'Favrile' Glass." *The Studio* 14 (June 1898): 15–21.

"Watercolors by Louis C. Tiffany." *American Magazine of Art* 13 (1922): 258–59.

Photograph Credits

The author and publisher wish to thank the museums, galleries, libraries, and private collectors who permitted the reproduction of works of art in their possession and supplied the necessary photographs. Principal photography is by Richard Goodbody and David Robinson. Photographs from other sources and by other photographers (listed by page number) are gratefully acknowledged below.

Courtesy John Michael Burlingham: 10, 12, 13; Christie's Fine Art Auctioneers, New York: 106; Joseph Crilley: 19; Theodore Flagg, Winter Park, Fla.: 23; courtesy The Great Gatsby, Atlanta, Ga.: 68; Phil Moloitis: 46; courtesy Neil Auction Company, New Orleans: 40, 41; courtesy Sotheby's, Inc., New York: 91–93, 102, 122 top; courtesy Janet Zapata, New York: 124, 125.

Index